John,

I hope you enjoy this book.

Best Regards.

Crafting Customer Value

Crafting Customer Value
The Art and Science

Peter Duchessi

Purdue University Press
West Lafayette, Indiana

Library of Congress Cataloging-in-Publication Data

Duchessi, Peter, 1953–
   Crafting customer value : the art and science / Peter Duchessi.
      p.   cm.
   Includes bibliographical references and index.
   ISBN 1-55753-231-1 (alk. paper)
   1. Customer loyalty.   2. Customer relations.   I. Title.
HF5415.525 .D83   2001
658.8′12—dc21   2001031745

Contents

Preface

In today's business world, the competitive forces that companies face, including speed, productivity, and innovation, reduce all products and services to commodities over time. This has adverse consequences, including the need to compete on price, reduced margins, and lower profits. How does a company compete in such a world? To be successful, all companies must create value for their customers. However, a significant number of companies fail to understand this point or struggle to create customer value.

Using a comprehensive framework, the Customer Value Framework (CVF), this book demonstrates the importance of delivering customer value, provides various strategies for defining customer value, and describes how to deliver customer value through operational excellence in the primary business, personnel, quality, and information systems that constitute a business. After introducing the framework, the book describes how to set clear business direction (a fully integrated and consistent set of goals, objectives, and associated strategies); how to identify customers and develop a full understanding of their needs and expectations; and how to formulate a customer value strategy, or value proposition, that attracts and retains existing customers, addresses the basis of competition, and delivers a profit to a company.

After a company decides where it wants to go and how it expects to add value to customers, it must design and implement the pertinent business, personnel, quality, and information systems. This book addresses each of these aspects. Concerning business systems, this book provides a detailed methodology for designing, or redesigning, business processes and a number of steps for successfully implementing a new process. With regard to personnel, it explains how to develop a loyal cadre of employees through employee selection, leadership, education and training, measurement, and compensation and recognition programs. The sections on quality describe the fundamental elements of quality programs, including quality concepts, techniques, and tools. Concerning information systems, this book demonstrates how to enable various business processes, such as order fulfillment, operations, and customer support and service, with information technology to create customer value innovations. Finally, this book concludes with practical advice on how to move forward and make progress, overcoming key obstacles that often derail even the best efforts.

Crafting Customer Value provides numerous examples to illustrate its points. Additionally, a number of short case studies demonstrate the application of frameworks, models, concepts, techniques, and tools. The cases are from notable companies, such as General Motors, Siemens, UPS, and Reader's Digest, and cover a variety of topics, including how to develop a cohesive strategy, redesign a business process, and effectively educate and train employees. Illustrations from several smaller companies demonstrate that all companies can benefit from the ideas presented in this book.

There is sufficient scope and scale between this book's covers to help managers realize a strong business posture that is based upon sound business direction, customer value, and operational excellence. Companies have two choices: wait for the competitive forces to speed their demise, or follow the guidelines in this book and realize their full potential and the associated profitability.

Acknowledgments

I would like to thank all of the people who helped me during the writing of this book. I especially thank my wife, Nancy, who was most patient and supportive as I completed the book. I dedicate this book to her.

CHAPTER 1

Creating Customer Value

"Everyone has become better at developing products. In robotics, the robot itself has become sort of a commodity. The one place you can differentiate yourself is in the service you provide."

—Eric Mittelstadt, former CEO and President,
Fanuc Robotics-North America

The key to success in today's business world is customer value. Companies must create value for their customers or face the consequences of declining customer loyalty, deteriorating market share, decaying profits, and the associated chaos that ensues. This concept is more than a business fad; it's the very essence of doing business. Yet a large number of companies just don't get it; they fail to understand the rudiments of value that are important to their customers and/or are incapable of creating value using the resources under their control. To be successful, companies have to provide quality products and services at fair prices, creating the impression of value and exciting customers about their products and services in the process. These imperatives require that a company understand its customers (perhaps better than they understand themselves) and manage its business as efficiently as possible.

The comprehensive and highly integrated method presented here for creating customer value gives companies the impetus and direction to unite multiple business functions around common goals and strategies; recognize the importance of focusing on customers' needs and expectations; comprehend the fundamental elements of customer value; and develop and implement the business, personnel, information, and quality systems required to deliver customer value. Through a top-down process, the approach helps

1

executives and managers develop and coordinate business goals, business
function objectives, and strategies; tie them to daily business activities; and
manage the detailed aspects of the business, quality, human, and information systems at their disposal. The approach can be portrayed as a pyramid,
the Customer Value Pyramid, with goals and strategies at the top and business,
personnel, information, and quality systems at the bottom (see Figure 1.1).
Anything less than this approach will not prepare a company to meet the
competitive forces and challenges that await in the future.

Competitive Forces

As trade barriers fall and deregulation matures, the number of competitors
that every business faces is increasing at an alarming rate. Excluding their
traditional competitors, many companies are faced with a number of new
challengers that didn't even exist a few years ago. For example, in the banking industry, nonbanks represent the chief competitors in both the corporate
and retail arenas. Concerning retail banking, a consumer can write a check

FIGURE 1.1
Customer Value Pyramid

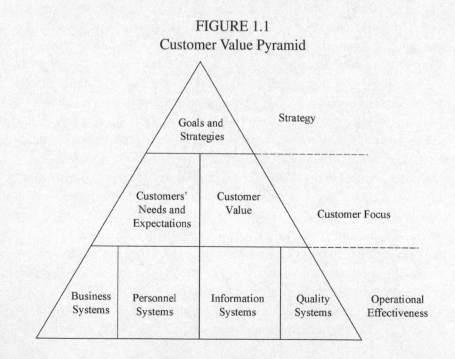

on a brokerage money market account, finance a car through GMAC (General Motors Acceptance Corporation), pay for daily purchases with a GE credit card, buy a house with a mortgage from an insurance company, and send a money order via Western Union. So who needs a bank? Banks are primarily responsible for this situation due to the questionable value of their products and services, lack of attention to customers' concerns, and inefficient business processes.

The spread of information technology is another potent force with which companies have to contend. Companies are using computers and communications technologies to provide more service to customers and optimize the processes that deliver those services. Consider the new business models that have emerged over the past few years with the growing presence of the Internet and World Wide Web (Web). The Web is a system with universal standards for storing, retrieving, and displaying electronic pages that contain text, graphics, and sound. Using the Web, companies offer speed, convenience, and personalization at levels that were unimaginable a few years ago. Dell Computer permits the customization and ordering of PCs online, which the company quickly assembles and ships. (Dell can assemble an OptiPlex desktop computer in just a few hours.)[1] Its direct approach to sales and service and its stellar operations have allowed the company to become the leading supplier of PCs to business customers, government agencies, educational institutions, and consumers.

Today, growing companies are more innovative than ever and the trend shows no signs of abating. Many companies are demonstrating continuous creativity in their product and service offerings, staffing arrangements, business processes, and information systems applications. As a result, product life cycles are shrinking and process innovations are proliferating. Companies are also better at adopting new innovations. The pace of innovation and change is so fast that what's new today is often old tomorrow. In some industries (e.g., electronics), the window of opportunity is just a few months. Being able to do it faster and with greater productivity is a constant pressure with which many companies must cope if they are to survive.

As some companies continue to get better, consumers learn to expect more, giving rise to the following paradox: If some companies can get it right, why can't others? Because of the large number of competitors and the ability to locate them easily, consumers are gaining the upper hand. For

example, at e-commerce hubs, buyers check prices and specifications offered by numerous suppliers around the world in real time. Instantly and
continuously knowing about the players, their products and services, and
respective prices helps buyers become highly effective at purchasing anything, including cars, insurance, and computers. Companies that enable
price comparisons to be made easily force everyone to lower prices, like it
or not. As companies and consumers get better treatment and better deals,
their expectations increase. Today's consumers are willing to spend money,
as evidenced by rising sales in almost all areas, but they demand better
value than their counterparts did in the past.

   Competition, overcapacity in a number of industries, advances in information technology, product and process innovation, wide availability of
information, abundance of smart consumers, and many other forces (for example, speed, productivity, and quality) mean that all products will become
commodities over time. This has devastating consequences, including the
need to compete on price, the increased potential for weak margins, and the inability to create distinctiveness in the minds of customers. As a result, many
companies will be forced to find a better way, or risk falling by the way-
side. How does a company compete in a world like this? Not on price (if it
can help it), but rather through imaginative, high-quality services that increase the value of its offerings.

Avoiding Commoditization

All companies can find a way through the morass by adding original, high-
quality services to their offerings at fair prices that create value in the minds
of their customers. Companies can become market leaders by delivering superior customer value in one of three ways: increase product and service
quality, lower prices, or do both simultaneously. The latter is the most difficult, yet the most financially rewarding option to pursue. Customers must
feel that they're receiving significant product and service quality for the
money they spend. Wal-Mart and Home Depot are national powerhouses
because they provide product and service quality at low prices, or considerable value to their customers. Service is a primary means for building customer value and earning higher profits as well. Companies will find that

- there are a number of services that are truly important to customers;
- quality service, a mix of service benefits and required performance levels, is heavily valued by customers; and
- quality service differentiates an offering sufficiently enough so that it doesn't become a commodity and strongly positions a company in a marketplace.

To be successful, companies must realize the importance of service and aggressively build quality services into their offerings. Aon Corporation, a Chicago-based insurance services company, offers a Web-based service that pulls together a database of the latest changes in government regulations and matches it with information on each client's operations. The service allows clients to better analyze their insurance needs and, as a result, effectively control their insurance costs.[2]

Through high-quality services and effective operations, companies can deliver superior, sustainable value to customers. Good companies that understand these concepts

- have a focus on customers and a clear understanding of their needs and expectations;
- offer a combination of product and service benefits and fair prices that constitute superior value to the customer; and
- aggressively manage the business processes, information technologies, and staff that are responsible for communicating, creating, and delivering customer value and allowing profitability at the same time.

The less astute companies may have to rethink their offerings and service delivery systems. Incremental changes, including simple line extensions and modest changes in productivity, are inadequate, especially in a world where a new business model, such as Dell's direct sales and service model, can topple an industry giant like Compaq in a few years' time.

Companies that excel at creating value strive to make their customers' lives easier and save them money. SpringStreet provides online lists of apartment rentals, as well as free quotes and deals on furniture, moving-truck rentals, and loan possibilities—all for free or at a discount. The company collects transaction and commission fees from a number of partners, including Visa and Ryder Moving Services, to cover the cost of its services.[3]

Quality Services Make Economic Sense

Creating and retaining loyal customers through quality services must be a high priority for all companies because these activities earn high returns. For example, a 5 percent increase in customer retention can increase profitability by between 25 and 50 percent. PricewaterhouseCoopers suggests that a 2 percent increase in customer retention has the same profit impact as a 10 percent reduction in overhead costs.[4] Moreover, the American Customer Satisfaction Index (ACSI), which first appeared in 1994, indicates a direct positive relationship between delighted customers and above-average stock returns.[5]

A satisfied customer, who perceives that he or she got a good deal and was treated well, will be a loyal customer. Loyal customers commit to a company, buy more, and continually return for additional products, services, and support. Companies that have a dedicated base of customers are resistant to commoditization and price wars because their customers are less susceptible to the competitions' entreaties. Thus, faithful customers represent long-term revenue and profit streams as their spending increases and accelerates over time. Betz Laboratories, a maker of industrial water-treatment chemicals, gives customers valuable expertise along with the chemicals it provides. Betz will help a company determine if the water it uses is safe for equipment as well as whether or not it meets EPA standards. Through these additional services, the company improves equipment uptime for its customers and saves them money. Betz engenders loyalty among its customers and, as a result, has become a significant supplier to many companies (e.g., AlliedSignal), doubling its sales in the process.[6]

As loyal customers become more familiar with the purchasing process, companies and their customers save considerable amounts of time and money. Dell's Premier Pages, customized Web pages for corporate customers, enables a customer's authorized employees to research, configure, and price the PCs they plan to buy. To minimize ordering errors, Premier Pages provides customer-specific information on system preferences, support details, and inventory management policies. With Premier Pages, Ford cut procurement costs by $2 million when it moved to online purchasing, and Dell benefited because it didn't have to hire as many order-entry people.[7]

According to conventional wisdom, it costs five times more to acquire a new customer than to retain an existing loyal customer, who purchases regularly. This is because a company often makes substantial investments in advertising, promotion, multiple sales calls, and channel development to get an initial trial purchase. Each time a loyal customer is lost to the competition, a company forfeits its initial investment and incurs a substantial cost to replace him or her. How many companies even consider this?

A study by the Technical Assistance Research Program (TARP) found that only 4 percent of dissatisfied customers ever complain to the company; the other 96 percent don't complain, they just go elsewhere. Moreover, 91 percent of dissatisfied customers never come back. These customers don't stop doing business, they just do it with a competitor. If this isn't bad enough, dissatisfied customers tell eight to ten people about their problem.[8] One customer is lost for every fifty who hear negative word-of-mouth advertising.[9] The business lost by not satisfying customers represents a high cost for any company. Companies not only forsake the initial investment required to attract customers, but the potential future revenue and profit streams those customers generate.

Companies That Don't Get It Right

Companies that don't commit to the idea of customer value and effective operations have a difficult time in the marketplace. Toyota's U.S. problems stem from poor customer service. Although its customers love the products, they're not happy with the way they're treated. Excluding the Lexus Division, customers rank the service at Toyota dealerships as just average. Complaints range from shoddy treatment to repeated trips to the garage to fix simple problems. As a result, just 42 percent of the company's customers return for another Toyota. To increase retention, Toyota is emphasizing customer service. It plans on teaching staff how to swiftly diagnose mechanical problems (reducing service times), and on letting customers order over the Web.[10]

Poor customer service has limited online retailing. According to one survey, 67 percent of online purchases are never completed, largely because many sites have made few provisions for customer service and support. Customer concerns range from inadequate product specifications to unreliable delivery. To be successful, online retailers have to emulate good business practice, including greeting new arrivals, offering service choices that move customers toward personal service, providing accessibility to staff for complicated questions, and supporting staff with the information and knowledge to field those questions.[11]

Other studies come to a similar conclusion: Superior customer service is vital for successful online retail sales. E-commerce companies may lose 60 percent of their customers every six weeks. Clearly, many online customers have little loyalty to existing sites or brands established over the Web. To cease the turnover and establish loyalty, many of these companies must build elements of quality service into their offerings to increase their overall value to consumers. Responsiveness, communication, and reliability are several important elements that customers appreciate. According to one study, 90 percent of online customers would make repeat purchases if they received more personalized communication and recognition. However, only 60 percent of the Web sites considered in the study respond to e-mails, and less than half of the sites provide additional information on products or promotions that are valued by customers.[12] The success of many online businesses and the promotion of their brands will depend on their ability to consistently provide high-quality online experiences and customer service. Although Internet sales were about $20 billion in 1999, could they have been much higher? Too many companies are losing money because of poor customer service, a correctable condition.

Companies That Get It Right

Landsend.com is an extensive Web site that provides customers with multiple ways to find products, determine style, and assess sizing. Through the site, customers can also arrange payment, shipping, and receipt of merchandise. Lands' End Live is a new service that will allow company representatives to contact customers via instant messaging or the telephone. Lands' End plans to use the service as a key differentiator. By assigning a representative to a customer, the company can browse with customers, answer basic questions, and provide advice. According to one analyst, the company has always been a customer service pioneer and is going the extra mile again. As a result of its attention to customers, outstanding service, and competitive prices (not always the lowest), Lands' End sells more clothing on the Web than anyone else, racking up $138 million in sales in 2000. The company delivers value; customers recognize it, are loyal, and reward Lands' End by spending money there.[13]

MBNA Corporation, the largest issuer of affinity credit cards, is committed to serving its customers. The company produces customized VISAs and MasterCards for over 4,000 affinity groups, including the National Education Association, Georgetown University, and Ringling Brothers. The company recognizes that its customers want good customer service quickly. Consequently, speed of service is an important priority. The company monitors its performance with a number of quality and speed measures (for instance, the telephone must be picked up within two rings). MBNA is constantly raising its performance standards to stay ahead of customers' rising expectations. The company's relentless pursuit of quality service has produced some spectacular results. In the first five years after going public in 1991, the return on equity climbed to 602 percent. Moreover, MBNA is able to retain about 98 percent of its profitable customers.[14]

Service is especially important for small companies that have to compete against the mass merchandisers who offer larger assortments of merchandise and lower prices. When a supercenter opens, the immediate first response for many small retailers is to lower prices. This couldn't be more wrong. The purchasing power of a Wal-Mart or Kmart just won't allow them to be undersold by small companies. Small independents can only survive by augmenting their offerings with services. Dechamps Incorporated, a regional chain of grocery stores, lowered its prices to thwart the opening of a Super Kmart. Price reductions received no recognition from customers. When the store focused on increasing the quality of products and services, sales went up and customers started returning.[15] Service can also prevent a company from being disintermediated. Realizing the Web would make it easier for resellers to bypass traditional distributors, MicroAge Incorporated, a computer distributor, transformed itself in 1995 into a service company, helping corporations with installation and training. The company even offers data on competitors' inventories to help customers when MicroAge is out of stock. With this approach, the company earns customer loyalty.[16]

Meeting the Challenges

To meet the competitive challenges and come out on top, a company must provide customer value. Conceptually it's straightforward, but in practice, it's difficult to do. An executive or manager must ask several questions:

- What do my customers consider to be real value?
- How do I systematically plan and control the business to deliver that value?
- Where does the business need to change, and how fast, in response to customer demands or service breakthroughs introduced by competitors?
- What are the methodologies and frameworks available for planning and controlling the requisite changes?
- What are the pertinent quality tools and techniques?
- How do I manage employees toward a successful service encounter?
- What are the relevant information technologies, how should I utilize them, and how do I implement them successfully?

To answer these questions and be successful at delivering customer value, companies must take a fully integrative approach. Myopic business concepts, strategies, and approaches will not suffice. To create value, a company must establish a clear direction toward customer value via relevant goals and strategies; pay close attention to customers' needs and expectations; develop a unique value proposition, which is a collection of product, service, and price benefits that constitute value for its customers; and manage the business's critical resources, namely processes, people, and information systems, which are primarily responsible for delivering customer value.

When a company commits to pursuing customer value, it must create a mission statement, a set of business goals, measurable business function objectives, and pertinent strategies at various organizational levels that make customer value a core concern of the business. At Southwest Airlines, customer service is a prominent part of the mission statement and is reflected in the company's goals and strategies. As a result, employees aren't confused about what to do on a daily basis; they're expected to serve customers and be results-oriented. Whether it's the best safety record, customer service record, or lower fares, the company is totally focused on customer value.[17]

In business, paying close attention to customers' needs and expectations is axiomatic. Companies have to be market-oriented and customer-driven. Yet the number of businesses missing the mark is legion. This is mysterious, especially when it happens in industries where there are ample opportunities to learn about customers.

In the mid-1990s, retailing lost touch with its customers. Selections were unsatisfying, prices were too high, service was unsatisfactory, and hours and locations were inconvenient. Several notable retailers, including Caldors, Bradlees, and Jamesway, became Chapter 11 casualties because they were out of touch with their customers' needs. The retailers who prospered gave customers what they wanted when they wanted it, and where they wanted it—all at the right price.[18] These successful companies, including Wal-Mart, Costco, and Home Depot, used their knowledge of customers, technology, and operational effectiveness to expand their offerings, lower the cost of doing business, and reduce prices.

Successful companies develop a unique customer value proposition that is commensurate with their direction and abilities and that satisfies—even delights—their customers. In many companies, such as the Wal-Marts of this world, being the price leader is the predominant factor of the value proposition. But it doesn't have to be. Companies can make service quality paramount and emphasize high-quality services that satisfy customers and allow the company to charge more, while still delivering considerable value to customers. In fact, one of the only ways for a company to compete against a competitor who is offering lower prices for comparable products is to add services. This increases the value of its offerings, satisfying the customer needs that competitors don't fulfill. Barnes & Noble's superstores turn book buying into a social and recreational experience. Shoppers can browse the merchandise and read in comfortable chairs while drinking a cappuccino. Although many of its books are available at lower prices elsewhere, Barnes & Noble gives customers numerous reasons to spend more time and money in its stores. This is in stark contrast to the more traditional mentality that discourages browsing.

After a company decides what it wants to be, what its customers need and expect, and which of those needs it wants to satisfy as defined by its value proposition, it must follow through with the best business, personnel, quality, and information systems for getting the job done (see Figure 1.2).

FIGURE 1.2
Primary Systems for Delivering Customer Value

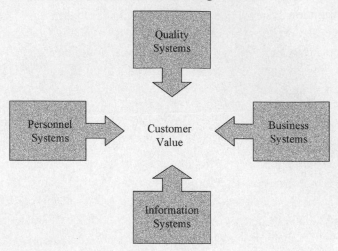

Companies can affect customer value creation through the business processes that fulfill customer orders, the people who work in or support those processes, and the quality and information systems that are an important part of all businesses today. Ill-conceived business processes will fail to satisfy customers and/or be too costly to operate. A system that is operationally ineffective can prevent a company from honoring its value proposition. With the correct business process design framework, companies can design, or redesign, their systems to be cost-effective and implement the appropriate quality techniques and tools to ensure high levels of product and service quality. The employees who staff or support a service delivery system are also important. Companies can't expect to engender loyal customers without a dedicated employee base. To develop a corps of employees who will effectively serve customers, companies have to lead, educate, train, nurture, empower, and reward their employees accordingly. Finally, information technology is a necessity for creating real value breakthroughs in all businesses. Companies can implement information systems with proven information technologies that add product and service enhancements to their offerings, improve almost any aspect of a business process from order entry to after-sales support, and assist employees as they serve customers.

In summary, companies need a systems perspective to make sure that all the pieces of the puzzle (from business goals to the installation of specific information systems that support those goals) make sense and fit perfectly together. Business processes, staffing arrangements, and information systems that don't add value and are inefficient should be replaced or eliminated. To ensure that value creation takes place, companies will undoubtedly make changes at various stages of their operations and customer value chains, from supplier to customer drop-off locations and from initial order entry to after-sales support and service, respectively. The approach provided here is comprehensive and totally integrative: it considers and integrates management plans, customers' needs and expectations, a company's employees, information technology, and business processes. It describes what has to be done as well as how to do it. It covers numerous aspects of the business from business plans to functional action plans and from the beginning of a business process to its end, weaving together ideas, people, and information systems in the process.

Companies must realize that customer value creation is a continuous process, considering the changes required to constantly fulfill customers' ever-increasing needs and expectations and to stay in front of the competition's ever-improving business, personnel, quality, and information systems. The approach presented here pulls together in one place the arguments, concepts, management frameworks, techniques, and tools for creating customer value. Many of the approach's ideas are new; however, some of them are not. Because the approach integrates and harmonizes the many facets of value creation, it will give executives and managers the know-how to make their businesses more valuable to customers and more profitable to themselves.

Management Directives

There are several key points that managers can extract from the advice and examples.

- Use customer value to confront the menacing world. The competitive forces created by competition, overcapacity, information technology advances, smart customers, and so on reduce all products and services to commodities over time—a frightening notion. Companies can survive commoditization by delivering superior customer value. To be successful, companies must offer a clever combination of product and service benefits at fair prices that create value in the minds of customers. If they can't, they shouldn't be surprised when their customers defect to the competition for a better deal. Companies that don't understand this concept will have difficulty in getting customers to consider them, experience high customer turnover (i.e., low customer retention rates), eventually be forced to compete on price, and watch their growth and margins diminish.

- Build customer value through services. One sure way to increase customer value is to enlarge the service dimensions of basic product and service offerings. Quality services can elevate a company's offerings and increase their value to customers. Through quality services, companies can create and retain loyal customers, increasing revenues, reducing costs, and improving profits. The economics of increasing value through quality services suggest that any other type of behavior would be irrational.
- Recognize that creating customer value isn't easy. Companies without a history or culture of creating customer value may have to radically alter their businesses. Companies must implement and aggressively manage congruous service delivery systems, quality systems, information technologies, and staffing arrangements needed to deliver their notion of value. Considering that customers' needs and expectations, competitors' actions, and technology applications are constantly changing, companies must constantly reevaluate their value propositions to ensure that they're relevant, changing the composition of the business processes, people, and technology to keep pace. Value creation is a continuous process.
- Don't use shortsighted and narrow approaches. Companies need a comprehensive, integrated approach to establish the correct plans. They need to understand customers' needs and expectations; derive a value proposition; and manage the business process, information technology, quality systems, and personnel systems required to deliver their value proposition. Anything less than the approach presented here, which integrates management goals and strategies, knowledge of customers' needs and expectations, value propositions, business, information, quality, and per-

sonnel systems, will leave management unprepared to address the competitive forces and deliver the value expected by customers.

Notes

1. E. Brown, "America's Most Admired Companies," *Fortune,* March 1, 1999, pp. 68–73.

2. H. Green, "Throw Out Your Old Business Model," *Business Week E.Biz,* March 22, 1999, pp. EB22–EB23.

3. Ibid.

4. J. A. Murphy, "The Logic of Customer Retention," <http://winningbusiness archive.com/winningn2/wb1998s/sup1a1.htm>, accessed March 29, 2000.

5. L. Grant, "Your Customers Are Telling the Truth," *Fortune,* February 16, 1998, pp. 164–66.

6. M. Magnet, "The New Golden Rules of Business," *Fortune,* February 21, 1994, pp. 60–64.

7. E. Brown, "America's Most Admired Companies," *Fortune,* March 1, 1999, pp. 68–73.

8. J. Plymire, "Complaints as Opportunities," *Journal of Services Marketing* 5, no. 1 (Winter 1991), pp. 61–65.

9. "Making Complaints Pay," *Management Decision* 32, no. 5 (1994), pp. 55–56.

10. B. Bremner, L. Armstrong, K. Kerwin, and K. Naughton, "Toyota's Crusade," *Business Week,* April 7, 1997, pp. 104–114.

11. L. Grant, "Spotty Service Hinders Online Retailing," *USA Today,* June 1, 1999, p. 8A.

12. D. P. Puzo, "E-commerce Baffled by Customer Service Concept," *Forbes,* July 6, 1999, <www.forbes.com/asap/html/99/0706/feat.htm>, accessed March 23, 2000.

13. P. Patsuris, "Lands' End Goes Live," *Forbes,* September 14, 1999, <www.forbes. com/tool/html/99/sep/0914/mu8.htm>, accessed March 23, 2000.

14. J. Martin, "Are You as Good as You Think You Are?" *Fortune,* September 30, 1996, pp. 142–52.

15. C. Y. Coleman, "How Grocers Are Fighting Giant Rivals," *Wall Street Journal,* March 27, 1997, pp. B1, B12.

16. R. D. Hof, "What Every CEO Needs to Know about Electronic Business: A Survival Guide," *Business Week E.Biz,* March 22, 1999, pp. EB9–EB12.

17. J. Huey and G. Colvin, "The Jack and Herb Show," *Fortune,* January 11, 1999, pp. 163–66.

18. M. Kuntz, L. Bongiorno, K. Naughton, G. DeGeorge, and S. Andersen, "Reinventing the Store: How Smart Retailers Are Changing the Way We Shop," *Business Week,* November 27, 1995, pp. 84–96.

CHAPTER 2

Seeing the Big Picture

"Keeping the idea simple and sticking with it are key, . . . most smart people tend to complicate things."
—James M. Sweeney, former CEO, Coram Healthcare Corporation

Scores of issues confront managers on a daily basis, from defining long-term strategic direction to ensuring the daily provision of quality products and services through their companies' business processes. To effectively deal with these issues, managers require a comprehensive and integrative framework for determining where the company should go; identifying what customers need and expect; determining the product and service benefits that impart customer value; and developing the business, personnel, quality, and information systems that deliver value to customers. Such a framework would integrate strategy formulation, customers' needs recognition, and the implementation of advanced business systems to develop and maintain a state-of-the-art company.

Frameworks are valuable when they're easy to comprehend, flexible (i.e., used to develop a new service-oriented business from scratch or implement "on the fly" improvements to an existing business), and result in success. Moreover, because all companies develop their own inertia, good frameworks provide opportunities for both dramatic and incremental changes in the way companies conduct business so that nothing remains stable for long. The comprehensive and integrative Customer Value Framework presented here satisfies these criteria. It consists of seven steps (see Figure 2.1).

1. Determine business direction
2. Identify target customers and assess their needs and expectations
3. Define a value proposition

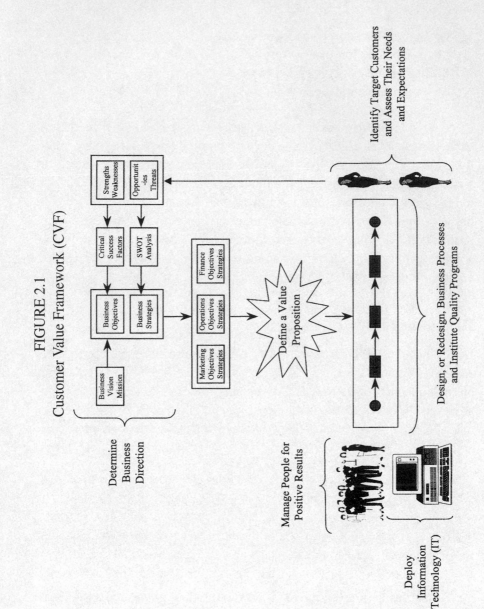

FIGURE 2.1
Customer Value Framework (CVF)

18

4. Design (or redesign) business processes
5. Manage people for positive results
6. Institute quality assurance programs
7. Deploy information technology (IT)

A complete understanding of business direction; customers' needs and expectations; a value proposition; and the required business, human, quality, and information systems collectively represent a business concept, or business model. When a company implements a business concept that delivers superior customer value through an operationally effective system, it has a "winning" approach that engenders customer loyalty and earns high profits. Following is a brief overview of the CVF's seven steps. It provides a macro perspective before moving on to succeeding chapters, which develop each part of the CVF completely.

Determine Business Direction

Determining business direction involves defining a vision and mission that are devoted to serving customers, specifying a set of achievable business goals and business function objectives, and developing strategies to accomplish those goals and objectives. Collectively, these elements give a company purpose and direction, allowing all employees to answer the following important questions:

- What is our business?
- Who are our customers?
- What are the customers' needs and expectations?
- What do we expect to accomplish?
- What actions will we undertake in each functional area of the business?
- How will we evaluate and control our performance?

At the business level, having a vision, mission, goals, and associated strategies provides a focus for the business. Without a focus, even a laser-like focus, companies can take on too much for the sake of increasing sales revenue and lose their way, often running aground. For example, Sears tried to be too many things to too many people and faltered, with consequent financial losses and disruptions in operations across the chain. Only when management decided on what the company should be and where it should go did a turnaround commence, primarily because management provided a focus for the company.

The process of developing a set of meaningful business goals and strategies, as well as specific business function objectives and strategies, involves two related analyses:

1. SWOT (strengths, weaknesses, opportunities, and threats) analysis,[1]
2. CSF (critical success factor) analysis.[2]

The SWOT analysis consists of an internal analysis of a company's strengths and weaknesses and an external analysis of existing and potential opportunities and threats in the context of the company's customers, competition, technology, society, and government. The internal analysis helps a company surface what it does well and not so well; the external analysis identifies external events, including promising market opportunities, shifts in customer needs and expectations, technological developments, competitors' actions, and government regulations that present opportunities or pose threats to the company.

With an understanding of what it takes to be successful in the external environment, a company can articulate a set of CSFs that determines success or, conversely, failure. The CSFs and mission provide a basis for defining a set of business goals. In addition to the mandatory profit, return on investment (ROI), and market share goals, these goals should address the basis of competition in and the competitive forces shaping the current business world (e.g., speed, innovation, productivity, and service) and allow a company to differentiate itself from the competition. By juxtaposing strengths and weaknesses with opportunities and threats, a business can formulate business strategies for realizing its mission and achieving its business goals. For example, a company can craft a strategy that maximizes its strengths to take advantage of opportunities and thwart existing and pending threats.

A business's goals and strategies have direct implications for each of the business's primary functional areas, including sales, operations, and customer service. In each functional area, managers must ask the following question: "What tasks and activities are essential for achieving the company's goals?" During the business planning process, the managers of each functional area answer this question in their plans. A plan includes business function objectives and strategies; action plans or programs (statements of the activities and technologies needed to pursue those objectives and strategies); special projects for initiating changes in organizational culture, business processes, and quality programs; and associated budgets for the action plans or programs and special projects. Thus, the plans or programs and projects actuate a company's business goals and strategies.

Identify Target Customers and Assess Their Needs and Expectations

Without customers there is no business. Companies do well when they define their target customers, develop a solid understanding of their needs and expectations, and meet or exceed those needs and expectations. Consequently, there are three basic questions that companies need to answer:

1. Who are our customers?
2. What do they need and expect?
3. How well does the company satisfy customers' needs and expectations?

Defining a group of customers to pursue, or a target market, is critical to avoid guessing at what's appropriate in terms of product and service offerings. Some companies stumble because they've lost track of whom they're serving. Targeted customers define an offering's attributes, as well as its price. They also give companies insight into the products and services that could be successful in the marketplace, allowing companies to exceed customers' expectations with new product and service offerings that may not be articulated by customers.

When the actual performance of a service meets or exceeds customers' expectations, customers are satisfied; anything less isn't acceptable. Meeting customers' expectations shouldn't be viewed as "we're doing great"— it should be viewed as the minimally acceptable standard. There are two predominant reasons for not living up to customers' expectations:

1. significant misapprehension of customers' needs and expectations, and
2. inability of business processes to provide customer-stipulated products and services at desired performance levels.

Generally, customers want to have it their way: highest quality, at the lowest price, as quickly as possible. Companies cannot become customer-driven without understanding the detailed needs and expectations of their customers along each of these, as well as potentially other, dimensions. Needs and expectations assessment is especially difficult because customers' needs and expectations are dynamic, changing over time in response to competitors' actions and the shifting demographic and psychographic profiles of the target market. Although having a winning (albeit proprietary) technology, Apple Computer failed to keep pace with their business customers' evolving needs for open systems, minimum hardware costs, and a broad range of business software.[3]

Define a Value Proposition

With a firm understanding of its requirements (as described by its mission, goals, and strategies) and of its customers' needs and expectations, a company can define a value proposition as the strategy for how it expects to deliver superior value to customers and earn a profit. Here, value is defined as a collection of product and service benefits at a reasonable price. It's a simple concept! Good companies offer a clever combination of various product benefits (including performance, conformance, and aesthetics) and service benefits (including reliability, responsiveness, and competency) at fair prices that win and retain targeted customers and deliver significant profits in the process. A company's value proposition determines why customers decide in its favor rather than go elsewhere for products and services. Companies can increase value in three ways:

1. emphasize product and/or service benefits, while leaving prices constant;
2. reduce prices, while offering competitive product and/or service benefits; and
3. do both: enhance product and service benefits and lower prices simultaneously.

Companies can succeed with any of these value strategies as long as their combination of product quality, service quality, and price creates value in the minds of customers.

Companies that select the first strategy build exceptional product and service quality into their offerings. For example, to compete against the mass merchandisers and category killers that are overrunning the landscape, many of the nation's independent nurseries are beginning to offer exceptional service to their customers, including stocking plants suited for local conditions, providing advice to ensure longevity, and hosting special events. Brackens' Nicholson-Hardie Nursery and Garden Center makes house calls, providing advice on how to water and fertilize. Homestead Gardens holds an herb festival with local chefs demonstrating how to prepare herbal marinades and garnishes. These companies may charge upscale prices, but they deliver exceptional value in the minds of their customers and are profitable as well.[4]

Companies that employ the second strategy—reducing prices and leaving the product and/or service quality factors constant—recognize that prices are sticky on the downside unless they're operating cost-effective systems. Consequently, they implement business processes that are the least cost (or among the lowest cost) so that they can reduce prices and still make money. For example, online brokerage houses are offering exceptional service at transaction fees that blow away traditional trading fees. Charles Schwab provides account information, company-specific histories, and trading functionality at fees that are four to five times less than those offered by a conventional broker. By substituting information systems for people, Schwab has lowered its cost position without forsaking the information and services expected by customers and traders.

The truly exceptional companies choose the third option: enhancing product and service benefits and lowering prices simultaneously. They offer the best product and the best service at the best price; they have a superior business model that creates value for customers and delivers profits to owners. Wal-Mart is one paragon with this approach. The company offers brand-name merchandise, has excellent customer service, and is the price leader in its industry. Additionally, the company has designed its business systems, including in-store operations, logistics, and marketing, to outpace the competition, giving it the ability to pass on cost savings to its customers in the form of lower prices. This approach is clearly the best—it delivers the greatest value to customers. However, it is the most difficult approach because it requires companies to achieve a state of operational effectiveness that results in lower costs, while still providing product and service benefits that customers perceive to be superior for the price.

The approach chosen by a company has direct implications for the service delivery systems it puts into play; the way it educates, trains, and motivates employees; the quality assurance programs it deploys; and the information technology it utilizes. All of these elements must come together gracefully so as to implement a value proposition that pleases customers and realizes the company's goals and strategies.

Design (or Redesign) Business Processes

A business process is a sequenced collection of activities. Order entry, customer service, and invoicing are examples of business processes. To design, or redesign, their business processes for greater customer value, companies can adopt the following six-step program:

1. set business direction,
2. identify core service processes,
3. develop deep process knowledge,
4. learn from world-class standards,
5. design a new service process, and
6. implement the new service process.[5]

Without a methodology for pursuing changes to a service delivery system, companies can spend a lot of money and have nothing to show for it. The business literature is replete with stories about companies that have fallen far short in trying to reengineer themselves. These six steps constitute a thoughtful approach that can help a company avoid the pitfalls and develop effective and efficient service delivery systems.

Manage People for Positive Results

Many business processes involve people who interact with customers to deliver or facilitate the delivery of products and services, beginning with order entry and carrying through to after-sales customer service. The point where customers encounter employees is extremely important and must go well, because customers form opinions about the overall quality of the service and the company during the course of the encounter. Jan Carlzon, former CEO of Scandinavian Airlines System (SAS), calls this point "the moment of truth." In fact, people are a critical factor in delivering high-quality service. Every employee is a different "facet" of the business, and every employee can potentially gain or lose customers. Companies need a motivated group of employees who are committed to the customer. But how does a company accomplish this? How does a company create a customer-oriented culture? Companies can affect the success of service encounters and develop a positive culture by the way they

- select employees,
- lead them,
- nurture them,
- educate and train them,
- empower them,
- measure their performance,
- provide feedback, and
- compensate them.

Through the selection process, companies are able to cull people who genuinely like other people, will take the initiative, are capable of solving customers' problems, and are capable of working in a group environment. By providing the correct leadership, a nurturing environment, and education and training, service-oriented companies develop strong customer-oriented cultures, where employees are empowered to initiate and sustain processes that put the customer first. Measurement and feedback systems allow employees to understand how well they're performing vis-à-vis customer satisfaction objectives. Companies can also implement reward programs linked to those objectives to ensure that employees will focus on the attainment of those objectives. According to Jack Welch, CEO of GE, job rewards have to be in the soul and in the wallet.[6]

Institute Quality Assurance Programs

Quality assurance is the discovery and elimination of quality problems from a business process. With a quality assurance program in place, companies can reduce the negative impact of nonconformance—including expediting charges, unplanned service, and customer complaints—which eventually leads to customer defection. Companies can implement Total Quality Management (TQM), a comprehensive program that emphasizes excellence in all areas of a business, or they can adopt a more moderated approach, which applies several TQM techniques to their business processes, including

- check sheets,
- pareto diagrams,
- cause-and-effect diagrams,
- histograms, and
- control charts.

These techniques help employees identify the factors that are responsible for defects in products and services. They provide graphical displays of performance over time and help employees diagnose the causes of poor performance. With knowledge of the causes of nonconformities, managers and service employees can take steps and execute actions to eliminate them and prevent their reoccurrence.

Deploy Information Technology (IT)

Advances in computer hardware, computer software, and communications technologies have allowed companies to reengineer service delivery systems and achieve amazing service breakthroughs. In every breakthrough, computer and communications technologies are the enabling elements and, as a result, they have penetrated almost every activity of the value chain, including logistics, operations, marketing/sales, and after-sales service.

Cisco Systems, a maker of networking equipment, uses its network to link suppliers, contract manufacturers, and assemblers, speeding the flow of merchandise to its customers. Via the Cisco network, outside contractors monitor incoming orders and ship the requisite hardware to customers later in the day, without Cisco even touching the box. By outsourcing production of 70 percent of its products, the company has quadrupled output and reduced time to market by two-thirds, down to six months.[7]

Many companies have used the Internet to develop completely new business models. For example, Autobytel.com has transformed the entire process of purchasing cars and trucks. The company acts as an intermediary between the customer and dealerships that it accredits. At the Autobytel. com Web site, shoppers can obtain information about a vehicle, including vehicle reviews, dealer incentives, and vehicle specifications; compare various vehicles and their prices; and purchase, lease, or finance a vehicle. The Web site passes on a purchase request to an accredited dealer, which sends the customer a quote in about 24 hours. By taking advantage of Internet technologies, Autobytel.com is capable of providing all the services of a conventional sales agent with more speed and convenience—and reach a worldwide audience of potential customers. Moreover, Autobytel.com has a service that reminds registered customers of recommended service visits, schedules service appointments, and keeps track of a vehicle's service history. Other products and services provided by Autobytel.com include

- auto insurance and warranties,
- after-market products available through Autobytel.com's accredited dealers, and
- auctions for retail and wholesale markets.

The company aims to become the single marketplace for all automotive needs. In the process, Autobytel.com has improved customer satisfaction with online buying services and has increased sales and reduced overhead at accredited dealerships.

Information technology is capable of transforming how companies sell products and services in a host of industries. However, enabling business processes with computer technology is not a straightforward process. In fact, managers consider only 16 percent of information systems implementations successful.[8] To be successful, companies need managerial and organizational support and an implementation process that includes formal project planning, thorough requirements analysis, and ample education and training for managers and end users. The implementation of a large system doesn't have to be the most important priority in a company, but it does have to be at least as important as other business activities.

Applying the Customer Value Framework: The GM Experiment

Using the CVF, GM has developed the Mobile Network Service Function (MNSF), a new approach to automotive service in which technicians in specially equipped vans will perform vehicle maintenance and minor repairs at customers' residences or workplaces.[9] The impetus for the MNSF came from a GM business strategy to attract or retain new and existing customers by providing uncompromising satisfaction throughout the ownership experience. The dealerships share this strategy as well.

Although all customers could benefit from the new service, GM initially chose the upscale market because the customers in this segment generally have greater demands on their time and greater appreciation for convenience in service offerings. GM recognized that customers in this target market have several needs, including

- timely maintenance to protect and minimize the operating expenses of their investments,
- convenient and reliable service that minimizes the demand for time on their busy schedules, and
- avoidance of unproductive waiting time at repair facilities.

In defining a value proposition, GM distinguished between technical quality (i.e., what's delivered) and service quality (i.e., how it's delivered). With regard to service quality, GM's value proposition includes up-front, competitive pricing (so customers are fully aware of all repair or maintenance costs prior to making an appointment) and the following service benefits.

Service Benefits	Detailed Characteristics
Reliability	Accurate billing
	Accurate record keeping
	Correct and "error-free" maintenance and repair
	Effective time scheduling and efficient operating practices
Responsiveness	Prompt response to customers calls and e-mail
Access	Availability via an 800 number and e-mail
	Minimum wait time to speak with customer service coordinators
Credibility	Elimination of hard sell tactics
	Trustworthiness via existing dealerships' names and manufacturer-backed reputations

Courtesy	Polite, respectful, considerate, and friendly personnel
	Personable appearance
	Maximum consideration for customers' property

Pricing of services occurs in three categories:

1. competitive service pricing for common service offerings (for instance, oil and filter changes, tire rotation, and state inspections),
2. maintenance or menu service pricing for services based on mileage or expired time and manufacturer recommendations (for instance, belts, air filters, and spark plug replacements), and
3. repair service pricing for services that correct mechanical malfunctions (for instance, water pumps, alternators, and wiring).

To promulgate the MNSF service concept, participating dealerships explain the concept as part of the new-vehicle delivery process and advertise it via direct mail, newspaper, radio, and television. Moreover, dealerships can use the service van as a moving billboard with graphics that include an MNSF dealership's name, phone number, and e-mail address.

Order entry and a fully equipped van constitute the service delivery system. Concerning order entry, via a toll-free number, customers will contact a service coordinator, who will complete a service order and schedule an appointment. GM summarizes the process with five "road-to-the-sale" steps:

1. give a friendly greeting,
2. listen to the customer's concerns,
3. restate the customer's concerns,
4. present recommended manufacturer maintenance, and
5. ask for the business.

Via the Internet, customers can complete a service order by themselves. For these orders, coordinators will contact customers to verify certain information and confirm appointment times. Coordinators will also respond to e-mail messages from customers about service issues. Coordinators will determine the amount of time for a repair or maintenance service and dispatch a technician.

The technicians are experienced mechanics who travel to customers' sites in vans that have equipment, tools, and manufacturer parts. A sample of the equipment and tools follows.

Service/Repair Categories	Tools/Equipment Descriptions
Air bag	Air bag adapter
Antenna	Antenna bezel socket
Battery	Charger and cables
Cooling system	Coolant flush machine and testers
Exhaust	Jack and stands
HVAC	Manifold gauge/leak detector

The cost of the van, tools, and equipment exceeds $50,000.

To promote a positive service encounter, the selection of technicians from dealerships will be based on a number of criteria. Technicians must have and demonstrate proper appearance, a pleasant attitude, good communication skills, self-motivation, a good driving record, proficiency in repairs, and a professional behavior. Additionally, the technician should have a minimum of two years of dealership experience, possess extensive product knowledge, and perform well in role-playing exercises. Prior to customer contact, dealerships will provide education and training in the areas of formal problem-solving, communication skills, customer relations, program guidelines, and quality assurance. With this extensive preparation, dealerships can empower technicians to maximize customer satisfaction.

To evaluate service quality, customers can complete an eight-question card. The card includes the following questions, which require a yes or no response, five-point rating, or Likert scale rating.

- Was the repair or maintenance done right?
- How satisfied were you with the explanation of repairs given by the technician?
- Overall, how satisfied were you with the service?

To foster direct feedback on quality, GM and participating dealerships will support an 800 number and e-mail for customers who have complaints.

The MNSF service concept uses conventional communications technology to link technicians and coordinators. Technicians will be armed with cellular phones and pagers. Computers at dealerships will provide scheduling and routing support for the coordinators. For example, from currently available dealership systems, coordinators can generate all repairs for the day to be assigned to technicians. For each customer, coordinators will enter data, including vehicle type, service dates, and vehicle mileage. Dealerships will analyze the data to identify repeat customers, determine customers' driving habits, and recommend maintenance, making them proactive in terms of generating revenue.

Management Directives

Several imperatives arise from the previous overview and its examples.

- Visualize the big picture. Managers often don't conceptualize the steps required to successfully run a business and how they integrate together. Consequently, frameworks that are comprehensive and integrative in nature are extremely valuable. Good frameworks should provide management with a macro view of the business, while allowing the ability to focus on specific aspects of the business, including business goals and strategies, business planning, business processes, quality programs, and information technology.
- Have a clear focus. All companies require a clear focus to avoid going off course and the negative consequences that ensue. A vision or mission and an integrated set of pertinent business goals, strategies, and functional area business plans give a company the requisite direction it needs.
- Know the needs and expectations of the target market. All businesses should be based on satisfying, or exceeding, the needs of a targeted group of customers. This is difficult to do, considering that needs and expectations escalate over time. Customers want the highest product and service quality, at the lowest price, as quickly as possible. Yet a company can't begin to develop a customer value–oriented posture without a clear understanding of its customers.
- Formulate a value proposition. With an understanding of its business direction and customers' requirements, companies can define a value proposition or strategy for delivering superior value to customers. The

value proposition combines product and service benefits at a price that creates value in the minds of customers, giving them a reason to repeatedly choose one company's offerings over all others. There are various strategies, but offering the highest-quality products and services at the lowest possible prices is the ultimate, most difficult one. However, companies that can master it dominate their respective industries.

• Align business, quality, personnel, and information systems with the intentions of the company and its value proposition. Management's plans, customers' needs and expectations, and value propositions appear on paper. Nevertheless, they have direct consequences for the types of business, personnel, quality, and information systems that companies put into play. Companies have to implement effective and efficient business processes, use qualified personnel, enforce quality standards, and deploy the pertinent information technology that will allow them to deliver considerable value and return healthy profits. At this level, the decisions are less strategic and more operational in nature. Designing and operating systems of complex activities, people, and information technology provide the challenge. Yet managers can rely on proven programs, techniques, tools, and technologies for redesigning existing systems, ensuring service quality, and implementing information technology.

Notes

1. H. Weihrich, "The TOWS Matrix—A Tool for Situation Analysis," *Long Range Planning* 15, no. 3 (1982), pp. 54–66.

2. J. F. Rockart, "Chief Executives Define Their Own Data Needs," *Harvard Business Review,* March–April 1979, pp. 81–93.

3. A. J. Slywotzky and D. Morrison, "Insights Form a Falling Apple," *Wall Street Journal,* January 29, 1996, p. A14.

4. L. Lee, "If You Also Want to Buy a Crock-pot, This Isn't the Place," *Wall Street Journal,* August 26, 1997, pp. A1, A8.

5. This methodology resembles a six-step methodology suggested by Furey. See T. R. Furey, "A Six-Step Guide to Process Reengineering," *Planning Review,* March–April 1993, pp. 20–23.

6. J. Huey and G. Colvin, "The Jack and Herb Show," *Fortune,* January 11, 1999, pp. 163–66.

7. J. A. Byrne, "The Corporation of the Future," *Business Week,* August 31, 1998, pp. 102–06.

8. "Slow Start for C/S," *Datamation,* February 15, 1994, p. 15.

9. Currently, one Chevrolet dealership, Best Chevrolet, in the greater Boston area is testing the MNSF service model. Ron Bavier, GM Area Sales and Service Manager for the Boston area, wrote the initial business plan for the MNSF concept.

CHAPTER 3

Determining Business Direction

"The danger of the Internet is total confusion."
—Rupert Murdoch, Chairman, News Corporation

Both large and small companies need a framework for pointing themselves in the right direction and for integrating the planning and control aspects of their businesses with the daily activities that constitute their core business processes. Managers who are not rethinking their companies' direction on a regular basis and making the necessary changes to their businesses are running at a high level of risk. In a turbulent, changing world where new technologies and business models can reduce a company's products and services to commodities and make its business approach quickly obsolete, having clear direction is a necessity.

In the 1998 BT Challenge, where 14 racing yachts sailed around the world in the wrong direction (i.e., against prevailing winds and currents), the participants found that they needed a well-defined objective (e.g., finish in the top three on each leg of the race) to prepare themselves for the uncertain challenges they faced on a daily basis and to ultimately be successful.[1] Setting business direction has nothing to do with developing a lengthy five-year plan, as some managers think. In an ever-changing environment, a highly formalized, long-term business approach is doomed to failure. To make progress, a company needs an integrated set of short-term (for instance, one year in duration) business goals, business function objectives, and associated strategies that everyone in the company can focus on. By sticking with short-term goals, objectives, and strategies, companies can make corrections as needed and create and/or adopt new ways of doing things better.

35

In many companies, asking a dozen employees where the company is going will likely produce a dozen different answers, even at managerial levels. This is hardly the focus needed to move a company forward in a meaningful direction. Making sure a company has the right direction and focus is not an easy chore. The Business Integration (BI) model offers some assistance.[2] It's a framework for setting business direction and for ensuring that a company's operations are congruent with that direction (see Figure 3.1). It consists of the following seven steps:

1. define a vision and/or mission,
2. determine strengths, weaknesses, opportunities, and threats (SWOT),
3. identify critical success factors (CSFs),
4. determine business goals,
5. develop business strategies via SWOT analysis,

FIGURE 3.1
Business Integration (BI) Model

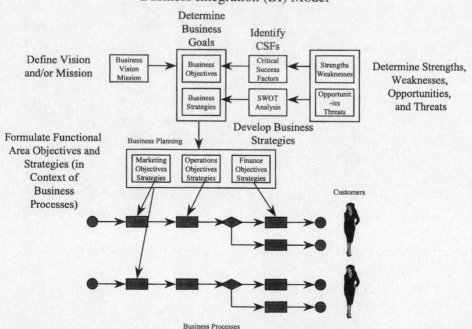

6. formulate underpinning business function and unit objectives, and
7. develop and institute supporting business function strategies in the context of business processes

Business goals and strategies serve as a guiding mechanism for detailed business function objectives and strategies. These objectives and strategies describe what will be done and how it will be done in each of the functional areas as those areas carry out part or all of a business process.[3] Understanding each step of the BI model and integrating them correctly is essential for a company's focus and the multitude of activities it performs.

Define a Vision and Mission

A company's vision and mission describe its purpose. Not all companies have vision and mission statements. Generally, they have one or the other. Good companies have at least one statement to direct their employees. The vision and mission statements should be short and sweet so employees can understand them, remember them, commit to them, and internalize them.

Succinctly, a vision statement describes why a company's employees go to work each day and a mission statement describes what they do when they get there. The vision describes where the company intends to be at some future, unspecified date. In most companies, it's a list of aspirations or high-level achievements that pertain to customers, suppliers, employees, and society. Alternatively, it can be just a simple statement. For example, Levi Strauss & Co., a maker and marketer of branded jeans and casual sportswear, has the following vision:

> Through relentless focus on consumers, innovation, and people, Levi Strauss & Co. will be the world's foremost authority in casual apparel.[4]

In contrast, the mission statement should answer the following questions.

- What is our business?
- Who are our customers?
- How do we add value to our customers?

Dell Computer's mission is

> . . . to be the most successful computer company in the world at deliv-
> ering the best customer experience in markets we serve. In doing so,
> Dell will meet customer expectations of

- Highest quality
- Leading technology
- Competitive pricing
- Individual and company accountability
- Best-in-class service and support
- Flexible customization capability
- Superior corporate citizenship
- Financial stability[5]

Senior management is responsible for creating a company's vision and
mission. Many companies use a facilitator to ensure that divergent thinking
takes place and to force convergence at a later stage, leading to a single con-
cise mission statement. In some companies, the chief executive files the mission statement away in his or her drawer: senior management knows about
it, but no one else in the company does.[6] Management needs to disseminate
the mission so that all employees know how to behave on a daily basis.

Even though the previous questions sound simple to answer, they can
be tough issues for companies to address. Yet a well-formed vision and
mission are necessities because they provide significant guidance in developing business goals and strategies.

Determine Strengths, Weaknesses, Opportunities, and Threats (SWOT)

All companies need to conduct an internal self-assessment of strengths and
weaknesses and an external analysis of opportunities and threats on a regular basis.[7] To be successful at running a business, managers need to take a
careful look at where the business stands today, be cognizant of any surprises
that emanate from forces outside of their companies that await them in the
future, and, in response, decide where their businesses need to go tomorrow.

The Self-Assessment

The self-assessment aims to identify a company's distinctive competencies (strengths) and surface areas that are responsible for poor performance (weaknesses) and require immediate attention. Strengths should be used to obtain goals, whereas weaknesses are limitations that prevent companies from achieving their goals.

Concerning strengths, almost all companies (including their competitors) can explain why they're successful. It could be due to a cost advantage (e.g., purchase and produce more efficiently); service distinction (for instance, 24/7 call center availability); or a technological competency (for example, advanced customer relationship management [CRM] software) that permits them to cross-sell and up-sell products and services (see Table 3.1). For example, one of Cisco's major strengths is its commitment and ability to make sure that all the disparate pieces of a customer's network mesh together.[8]

TABLE 3.1
Strengths of Several Prominent Companies

Companies	Competencies/Strengths
Wal-Mart	Information systems
	Inventory control
	Purchasing leverage
	Logistics systems
	In-Store operations
	Marketing strategy
UPS	Information systems
	Logistics systems
Gillette	Global reach
	R&D
	Innovation
E&J Gallo Winery	Marketing and sales
	Purchasing leverage

For most companies, the most difficult part of the self-assessment is identifying weaknesses. A competitive financial analysis is one (but not the only) way to proceed. In this type of analysis, a company can compare itself to an industry peer group, or a selected group of competitors, using a variety of efficiency, profitability, liquidity, leverage, and cost (e.g., cost of goods sold as a percentage of sales) measurements. For example, if a company's inventory turnover (an efficiency measure) is below the industry average, it means that the company may be mismanaging its finished goods, work-in-process, and/or raw materials inventory. By delving deeper and performing additional analyses, it may identify a swollen finished goods inventory. The work-in-process and raw materials turns are above the industry average, yet finished goods turnover is way below the industry average. Further investigation may reveal that the company's forecasting process is totally mismanaged, causing excessive finished goods inventory. In addition to financial results, companies can analyze or benchmark other areas, including cycle time, service quality, and other measurable success factors for their industries.

A careful self-assessment grounds a company in its current, internal reality. In some cases, the results are a blinding flash of what should be obvious. Yet it's amazing how many companies fail to take a frank look at themselves on a periodic basis or miss glaring deficiencies in their operations after careful evaluation.

The External Analysis

Good companies perform an external analysis of opportunities and threats on a regular basis. Nike is constantly reviewing how the world is changing and how it is reacting to it.[9] Opportunities are favorable situations in the environment that, if handled correctly, can result in significant returns, whereas threats are potentially damaging situations. Generally, senior managers take direct responsibility to know about the potential threats to their businesses and to encourage aggressive pursuit of new opportunities. To be sure, the world is discontinuous: global markets, incessant newcomers, digitization of products and services, deregulation, and constantly shifting consumer preferences are reshaping the business landscape. Consequently, companies need to perform the external analysis in the context of markets, competition, technology, government, and society.

With regard to opportunities, service-oriented companies need to be proactive at identifying ways to deliver greater value to customers by lowering costs, increasing product quality, and/or increasing service quality. One approach for identifying opportunities uses value chain analysis.[10] The value chain takes a systems perspective: it portrays a company as a collection of primary (e.g., inbound logistics) and secondary, support (e.g., human resource management) activities that admit inputs from suppliers, transform them into products and services, and distribute them to customers (see Figure 3.2). Through these activities, companies add value to their products and services, which is reflected in the prices they charge. If the cost of performing these activities is less than the price of selling the resulting product or service, then a company makes money.

By using the value chain, forward-thinking companies can examine a number of opportunities for delivering greater customer value. For example, they can use the value chain to evaluate computer applications that bring customers closer and/or lower costs (see Figure 3.3).[11] For example, by examining point-of-sale data, a grocery company can earmark loyal customers for rewards, including discounts, free items, and desirable coupons. In so doing, they can build a relationship with customers, minimizing defections and building the size of the shopping basket. Using an electronic communications system to exchange information, suppliers can electronically acquire their customers' manufacturing schedules so that they can align their operations with those schedules and deliver products and services just as they're needed. This approach reduces their customers' inventory position and improves throughput for both parties. By using the value chain to explore opportunities for themselves, companies can implement (long before their competitors do) technology-enabled service innovations that lead to greater customer satisfaction and higher profits.

Companies need to respond quickly to threats because, in some cases, business failure can be the end result. Expedia.com allows potential vacationers to roam hundreds of locations, communicate with travelers, and obtain write-ups and photographs of those locations. The Web site enhances the entire experience of trip planning to the point where it creates a serious

FIGURE 3.2
Value Chain Activities

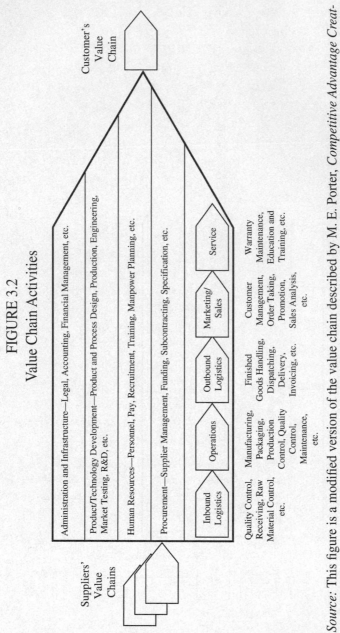

Source: This figure is a modified version of the value chain described by M. E. Porter, *Competitive Advantage Creating and Sustaining Superior Performance* (New York: Free Press, A Division of Simon and Schuster, 1985), and M. E. Porter and V. E. Millar, "How Information Technology Gives You a Competitive Advantage," *Harvard Business Review,* July–August 1985, pp. 149–160.

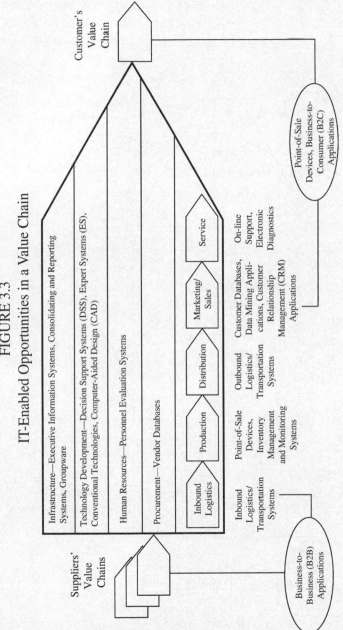

FIGURE 3.3
IT-Enabled Opportunities in a Value Chain

threat to traditional travel agencies and tour operators. Via Expedia.com, potential travelers can plan their vacation and make the necessary reservations. Additionally, there is nothing preventing the company from becoming a tour operator. For example, it can put together a vacation package, say a biking tour of Tuscany, float it over the Web, and book reservations. This new business model is a direct threat to traditional travel agencies and tour operators. Now, traditional travel agencies and tour operators must ask: "How are we going to get people to pay us money?" Computer technology makes it possible for companies that may not be considered traditional competitors to enter new markets and pose considerable threats to established businesses.

To monitor the external environment, companies can establish several measures to determine if the environment is changing in a direction that poses a threat or presents an opportunity. Consider newspapers that make their revenue through advertisements and the classifieds, which alone account for 40 percent of a newspaper's revenue. Classified Ventures is an online company that expects to establish national brand names in four classified segments, namely new homes, resale homes, autos, and apartments. Microsoft's CarPoint includes new and used car listings, reviews, and pricing. (In 1998, dealers were selling $80 million worth of autos a month through the site.)[12] In a world where advertisements and classifieds can be supplied electronically, a newspaper may consider one or more of the following technology measures to monitor its environment:

- number of Internet service providers,
- number of Internet subscribers,
- number of modems sold or extent of cable access,
- number of local and national sites with classifieds-type information, and
- number of companies (e.g., Reuters) offering news content over the Web.

All of these measures relate to entities that are outside of a newspaper's industry. The question, "What industry are you in?" becomes harder and harder to answer, especially when the sources of competition are newcomers with major service breakthroughs. These are not the only measures. A company needs just two or three good measures for each category, namely competition, society, government, technology, and market, to have a thermometer in the external environment. If the measures selected by a company signal red, the company should think through the threats posed to its traditional business model and act accordingly.

Identify Critical Success Factors (CSFs), Determine Business Goals, and Develop Business Strategies

For every business, there are a handful of critical success factors, or key ingredients of success.[13] Surprisingly, many companies don't take the time to discover and think through these factors. After performing the external analysis, a company is in a good position to articulate the CSFs that determine success in its industry. CSFs are the key areas where things must go right for the company; they're the areas that require management's constant attention. Typically, CSFs address the basis of competition. Some examples of CSFs in selected industries are

- global reach (media),
- service (telecommunication),
- knowledge (consulting),
- innovation (sports apparel), and
- quality (automotive).

Each CSF uncovered by a company has direct implications for the business goals that the company establishes for itself. With an understanding of its vision, mission, and CSFs, a company can define a unique set of business goals. For example, if service quality were an important CSF, then one goal would be to "become the industry (or world) leader in service quality." Johnson Controls, a manufacturer of automotive systems and building controls, has the following business goals.

- Customer satisfaction: We will exceed customer expectations through continuous improvement in quality, service, productivity, and time compression.
- Technology: We will apply world-class technology to our products, processes, and services.
- Growth: We will seek growth by building upon our existing businesses.

- Market leadership: We will only operate in markets where we are, or have the opportunity to become, the recognized leader.
- Shareholder value: We will exceed the after-tax median return on shareholders' equity of the Standard & Poor's Industrials.

At the business function level, these goals can be refined as a set of objectives that specify exact performance levels to be achieved in a specific period of time by each functional area.

Companies the world over have tried almost every conceivable strategy to outperform their competitors. Even though managers tailor their strategies to fit their unique capabilities and competitive and market situations, the strategies that companies pursue often fall into one of three general categories:

- cost leadership—become the low-cost producer or distributor,
- differentiation—incorporate product/service-enhancing dimensions for building greater value, or
- focus—select a market niche and dominate it via cost leadership or differentiation.[14]

Cost leadership and differentiation strategies alone may be insufficient in today's world, where target pricing and dynamic pricing are gaining acceptance and where competitors spring up and gain market share almost overnight with equally good, low-cost products. Whatever business strategy(ies) a company selects should result in a good and sustainable value proposition for customers. Customers don't care how big a company is, how well it is financed, or where it is located. They want to know how a company can save them money, give them a competitive advantage, and/or make their life easier. In most (and soon all) industries, the set of strategies that companies pursue will include both a differentiation and cost-leadership thrust. That's not to say that companies aren't making money by following either cost leadership or differentiation per se. Exceptional companies figure out how to do both simultaneously, providing real value to customers: the highest possible product and service quality at the lowest possible price (see Figure 3.4).

FIGURE 3.4
Competing on Value

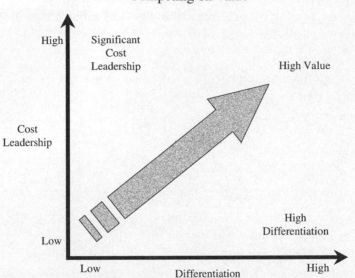

Source: This figure is a modified version of strategy formulation described by
M. E. Porter, *Competitive Advantage Creating and Sustaining Superior Performance* (New York: Free Press, A Division of Simon and Schuster, 1985).

Radio Shack is one company in the process of developing a value-oriented strategy in home connectivity. The company is positioning itself to help the technology-challenged household install and integrate a number of technologies, including Internet, cable or satellite TV, and local- and long-distance calling services. It plans to sell both high-quality private-label and brand-name products and provide expert advice on how to glue together a myriad of devices and technologies at competitive prices.[15] The company will create a Microsoft area in each of its stores to offer a number of Microsoft products, including MSN Internet Access, Windows CE-based hand-held devices, and Microsoft home networking software. Radio Shack selected Microsoft over other rivals because of Microsoft's software strategy for tying together all of the devices earmarked for the home of the future.[16]

With an understanding of its existing capabilities and market situation, as defined by strengths, weaknesses, opportunities, and threats as well as by its business goals, a company can begin devising specific strategies for

accomplishing its goals and delivering its mission. The process doesn't require a rocket scientist. In general, strategies are approaches that allow a
company to use its strengths to obtain its goals, overcome threats, and correct weaknesses. By juxtaposing strengths, weaknesses, opportunities, and
threats, companies can tease out pertinent strategies.[17]

For example, internal and external analyses of a small software development firm in the Mideast revealed that the company had several notable
strengths, namely a solid reputation for doing high-quality work, good con-
tacts in the region, and well-educated employees (see Figure 3.5). Even
though the workforce was technically strong, it had limited experience,
lacked significant project management experience, and relied heavily on
one type of database technology. Within the Gulf, businesses had a need
for integrated business solutions that combined reengineered business
processes with the correct enabling technologies rather than just computer
software, regardless of how well conceived it was. Additionally, the firm
was concerned that consulting firms with more complete sets of services
would enter the regional market. The company had just two objectives: become a leading software consulting firm in the Gulf and maximize profits.
Based on its internal capabilities and its analysis of the external environment, it developed the following four business strategies.

1. Develop a total systems approach for all business problems.
2. Develop the human resource component of the business.
3. Seek alliances with other software development firms that have project-
   management experience and complementary technical skills.
4. Form an alliance with a management consulting firm.

Without a set of business goals and strategies, functional areas and
units lack a well-defined path to follow. Even similar companies can take
different paths. American Express sells entitlement: members have special
services—the company will get a physician for its members in Rome any
time of the day. Visa sells ubiquity: "It's everywhere you want to be." Different strategies imply different types and levels of customer service and
determine how employees should think and act. In companies without substantive direction, everyone develops his or her own understanding of the
business, where it should be going, and how it should get there. Eventually,

FIGURE 3.5
Business Strategies

Business Goals:	Strengths (S): Reputation, good contacts, and good technical people	Weaknesses (W): Limited business and project mgt. experience, erratic assignments, and heavy reliance on one database management system
1. Become a leading software consulting business in the Gulf 2. Maximize profits		
Opportunities (O): Need for business solutions, need for systems integration, client-server applications, and object-oriented approaches	Develop a systems approach for business solutions, emphasizing client-server applications	Develop human reource component to build internal expertise
Threats (T): Strategic alliances to provide total business solutions	Form a strategic alliance with management consulting firms	Seek alliances with other hardware/ software firms

This figure is a modified version of TOWS Matrix described by H. Weihrich, "The TOWS Matrix—A Tool for Situational Analysis," Long Range Planning, 15 (2), 1982, pp. 54–66.

this leads to chaos and dysfunctional behavior. It is simply a case of people not being focused. Consequently, well-conceived business goals and strategies provide focus for tasks and activities that take place in each of a company's functional areas and business processes.

Formulate Business Function Objectives and Develop Supporting Strategies

Once a company decides where it wants to go, it has to develop best-in-class business processes to get there, because all businesses have a set of core business processes that drive them forward. Without them, the business wouldn't exist. Improvements in these processes lead to enhanced business performance and favorable outcomes for customers. Often these facts go unappreciated because management gets caught up in the vertical aspects of planning or, alternatively, management lacks an understanding of how to marry the vertical and horizontal perspectives of a business. The place for this union is at the level of business function objectives and strategies. If improvements are going to be made to a business process, it will be through the tasks (or objectives) assigned to each functional area that contributes to the process; the activities (as governed by strategies) they perform in accomplishing those tasks; and the tools, techniques, and technologies they utilize to implement the strategies.

During the business planning process, as marketing, operations, information technology, and other business function plans come together, managers must ensure that the objectives and strategies embedded in those plans consider the following areas:

- business goals and strategies,
- the gap between where a business process is today (baseline situation) and where it needs to be tomorrow to realize the business goals and strategies and deliver considerable value to customers, and
- scope of a functional area's contributions to business processes.

All companies have existing, or baseline, processes that collectively are the business. Examples include order entry, customer service, and new product or service development. These processes involve one or more functional areas. The functional areas perform several activities, sometimes at diverse locations, and with assorted amounts of technology, collectively imparting some level of performance to the process. In companies with network arrangements, other companies may conduct some of the activities. For example, a number of companies prefer to have UPS manage inventory and shipping activities. Ideally, the baseline processes meet customers' expectations and the internal requirements of a company as expressed by its business goals and strategies. Yet in most companies a "strategic gap" exists between where a process is today in terms of its performance and where it needs to be tomorrow to deliver value to customers, achieve business goals and strategies, and beat the competition soundly (see Figure 3.6). This is the point where the horizontal perspective of the business should take hold and horizontal thinking should replace vertical thinking. The gap is closed by an orchestrated set of objectives, strategies, and action plans that are carried out by each business function, subcontractor, and/or partner that contributes to the process.

Thus the objectives and strategies for a functional area must be set in the context of the business processes it affects, the strategic gaps in those processes, and the area's contribution to those processes. Understanding the scope of a functional area's contributions to a business process and the nature of its interface with other, involved functional areas is necessary for understanding what should be done, how it should be done, and who should do it.

Consequently, at this level, an objective is a task to complete in a certain amount of time. The task should support the business's goals and strategies, close business process performance gaps, and lead to superior outcomes for customers. All objectives should be SMART in nature.

- **S**pecific
- **M**easurable
- **A**ttainable
- **R**elevant
- **T**ime-bound[18]

Having a measurable objective is important, because, as the old saying goes, "What gets measured gets done."

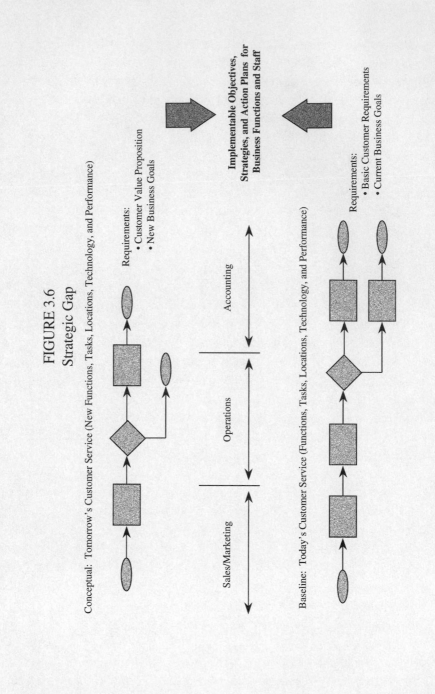

FIGURE 3.6
Strategic Gap

Conceptual: Tomorrow's Customer Service (New Functions, Tasks, Locations, Technology, and Performance)

Requirements:
• Customer Value Proposition
• New Business Goals

Sales/Marketing

Operations

Accounting

Baseline: Today's Customer Service (Functions, Tasks, Locations, Technology, and Performance)

Requirements:
• Basic Customer Requirements
• Current Business Goals

Implementable Objectives, Strategies, and Action Plans for Business Functions and Staff

At the business function level, strategies are broad statements for achieving an objective; they describe "how" to accomplish it. Each objective will have one or more strategies associated with it. The strategies add detail and govern the scope and scale of business function and unit activities as well as how they're managed. The primary roles of a business function's strategies are to

- support business goals and strategies, and
- achieve the business function's and affiliated business processes' performance objectives.

Additionally, the strategies suggest the implementation of specific techniques, tools, and technologies. The following illustrates how one company, a distributor of electronics, linked its goals, objectives, and strategies together.

One business goal was to become the industry leader in customer service. The company planned to differentiate itself through a strategy of accurate order entry, timely order filling, and exemplary service. One objective for sales was to attain 99 percent error-free orders in one year. The strategies associated with this objective were as follows.

Strategies	Tools, Techniques, and Practices
Provide an intelligent order entry graphical user interface (GUI)	Implement an enterprise resource planning (ERP) order entry module provided by a recognized ERP vendor (e.g., Baan, SAP, or JD Edwards)
Provide online hooks to remote inventory data	Develop order entry policies and detailed procedures for processing aspects of orders not addressed by the ERP system
Provide online credit checking	Provide generic education and specific training for using the ERP software

Achieve Full Integration and Consistency

As previously described, a company's strategic direction is an integrated collection of vision and mission statements; business goals and strategies; underpinning business function and unit objectives and strategies; and associated tools, techniques, and practices. The goals and strategies a company pursues and the scope and scale of its performance gaps determine the magnitude of its overall strategic initiative. Harmonizing the objectives and strategies across multiple organizational levels and various functional areas can be tedious and frustrating, especially when managers have multiple perspectives, are reluctant to state measurable objectives, and don't exercise strong leadership. Generally, there are opposing views, heated debates, and open disagreements. Yet a unified set of objectives and strategies is a necessity, because it transforms high-level strategic focus into a consistent set of detailed tasks and activities that fosters cooperation, coordination, and consistency across all functional areas and units. When properly applied by management, the BI model allows senior managers to form a hierarchy of goals, objectives, strategies, and tools (see Figure 3.7).[19] With tight linkages in place, management can reduce the chance of a business function straying from the direction established. Management should disseminate the contents of the hierarchy to all employees. This is the only way that employees will learn about what emanates out of a company's executive offices. By giving employees access to all of the hierarchy, they can develop an enlightened understanding of where the company is going, how to do their jobs, and what the critical performance measures are. This is especially important in companies with a lot of employees on the fringes in branch offices, on the road, or at partner sites. Because these people are not at the corporate office, they need to see the total picture so that they can cooperate fully and make the contributions expected of them.

Developing Business Direction at Jet Aviation Business Jets AG

Jet Aviation Business Jets AG is a leader in executive aircraft management and air taxi services in Europe, the Pacific Rim, the Mideast, and Africa. As part of its aircraft management services, Jet Aviation will help a client buy, staff, and maintain an aircraft over time. Through the air taxi service, clients can charter a private plane rather than fly a commercial airline. Jet Aviation's mission: "To be the world leader in the field of executive aircraft management."

The company's management develops business plans on a yearly basis. The plans contain tightly linked business goals, objectives, and strategies for a given year. Management bases every goal, objective, and strategy on

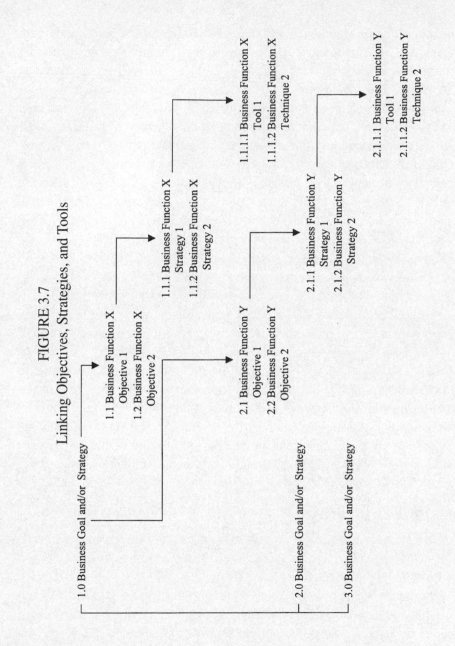

FIGURE 3.7
Linking Objectives, Strategies, and Tools

1.0 Business Goal and/or Strategy

1.1 Business Function X
Objective 1
1.2 Business Function X
Objective 2

1.1.1 Business Function X
Strategy 1
1.1.2 Business Function X
Strategy 2

1.1.1.1 Business Function X
Tool 1
1.1.1.2 Business Function X
Technique 2

2.0 Business Goal and/or Strategy

3.0 Business Goal and/or Strategy

2.1 Business Function Y
Objective 1
2.2 Business Function Y
Objective 2

2.1.1 Business Function Y
Strategy 1
2.1.2 Business Function Y
Strategy 2

2.1.1.1 Business Function Y
Tool 1
2.1.1.2 Business Function Y
Technique 2

55

a thorough understanding of its strengths, weaknesses, opportunities, and threats, CSFs, customers' needs and expectations, and assumptions about the market, competition, and technological developments (e.g., new cost-efficient planes) (see Table 3.2).

Senior management, key middle managers, and key staff establish a set of business goals and associated strategies, which everyone focuses on for the year. Two examples of past goals and strategies follow.[20]

Goals	Strategies
Achieve 100 percent customer retention	Improve customer service processes and aggressively follow up customer issues
Attain 95 percent customer satisfaction in the air taxi business	Incorporate customer feedback into all parts of the business
	Streamline the air taxi process

Completing the list are business goals on operating profit, aircraft financing, and employee satisfaction as well as strategies on forming strategic alliances, business process improvement, and implementation of quality programs and information technology. Each goal and strategy is for the current year and some are carried forward to succeeding years as necessary.

The company's primary business processes are

- customer service,
- dispatching,
- OMA/FSA (i.e., aircraft management),
- air taxi charter,
- sales,
- accounts receivable,
- accounts payable,
- new product development, and
- maintenance.

There are also a number of ancillary processes that support these core processes. With an understanding of the company's mission, goals, strategies, and

TABLE 3.2

Jet Aviation's Strengths, Weaknesses, Opportunities,
Threats, CSFs, and Customers' Needs and Expectations

Strengths	Weaknesses	Opportunities	Threats	CSFs	Customers' Needs and Expectations
Brand name	Staff turnover	Expanding Middle and Far East markets	Price competition	Customer service	Credibility (trust, fairness, honesty, etc.)
Financial strength	Poor follow-up after service	New airline products	Brain drain	Image	Security (privacy, confidentiality, safety, etc.)
Flexibility	Inefficient operations	New approaches to customer service	Technology gaps in operations	Value	Responsiveness (flexibility, speed of service, punctuality, etc.)

This table provides an incomplete listing of strengths, weaknesses, opportunities, threats, CSFs, and customer needs; some confidential information has been changed.

core processes, managers of the various business functions develop and commit to a set of SMART objectives and strategies for their respective areas. The primary business functions are maintenance, key account management, OMA/FSA, air taxi, personnel, administration, long-range dispatching, finance, and pilots and cabin attendants. Two examples of functional area objectives and strategies follow.

Maintenance

Objectives	**Strategies**
Maintain Jet Aviation–owned aircraft within budget	Obtain third-party quotes on large-scale maintenance projects
	Execute and report on monthly cost control steps
Attain 100 percent data accuracy on aircraft inventoried parts	Initiate a cycle count program for inventory control
	Supplement SAP inventory control–policies and procedure for all maintenance staff

Air Taxi

Objectives	**Strategies**
Achieve 90 percent customer satisfaction	Send customers a questionnaire on a quarterly basis
	Integrate electronic data-processing systems to avoid redundant operations and activities
Attain 100 percent correct invoicing	Automate the invoicing process

The objectives and strategies at this level support the business's goals and strategies and focus the energies of employees on specific deliverables. At times, the process of creating them is fraught with disputation, argumentation, and frustration. However, the end product is a set of unified and consistent goals, objectives, and strategies that govern detailed activities in each of the functional areas and business processes. Management reviews the company's progress on a continuous basis and any component of the plan may be altered to reflect changes inside or outside the company. For example, Jet Aviation made several changes to its plans in response to the Asian crisis when investments flowed out of many Asian countries, devaluing currencies and dramatically slowing the demand for executive jets and air taxi services.

Management Directives

The examples cited provide several lessons for managers.

- Make business goals and strategies provide a bearing. The vision and/or mission, business goals, and affiliated strategies provide business functions with substantive focus and guidance. Without them, functional areas are likely to develop their own, uncoupled approaches to business based on their limited perspectives. Well-conceived business goals and strategies are a necessity for getting the company to move in a unified direction.
- Set business function objectives and strategies in the context of business processes. Business processes perform the activities necessary for producing products and services. Innovative changes to these processes lead to enhanced business performance and better products and service outcomes for customers. Thus all functional areas must consider the business processes in which they partake when setting objectives and strategies. Functional areas need to think both vertically and horizontally to develop a set of specific objectives and strategies that achieve business goals through business process improvements. If the planning process is tight and goals as well as changing business conditions are properly communicated to employees, then consistent behavior will result. For example, if customer satisfaction is a business goal and it's declining, then sales, operations, distribution, and after-sales service will each be working on parts of the relevant business processes, depending on their relative contributions to those processes, with full knowledge of their coordinated roles and the critical interfaces. Through specific objectives, each area is highly focused on achieving business goals and

performing activities that improve business processes, using the best techniques and tools pertinent to those strategies.

- Set SMART objectives. Objects that are not *s*pecific, *m*easurable, *a*ttainable, *r*elevant, and *t*ime-bound will have no "teeth," will never be taken seriously, and will be superceded by other objectives, losing all sense of priority.
- Strive for full integration. The process of orchestrating goals, objectives, strategies, techniques, and tools is more likely to fail than not. Senior management is responsible for forming a unified set of plans and activities. By applying the BI model presented here, management can create the linkages among all areas and processes.

Notes

1. G. Colvin, "When It Comes to Turbulence, CEOs Could Learn a Lot from Sailors," *Fortune,* March 29, 1999, pp. 194–96.

2. The author developed the business integration model over a number of years and has successfully applied it to numerous companies.

3. In this framework, a goal is a specific outcome that a company strives to attain (e.g., increase market share, become the leader in customer service, etc.), and an objective is a measurable accomplishment for a specific period of time. Companies that are under a holding company may have business goals that are time-bound and measure specific accomplishments.

4. "Levi Strauss & Co. Mission, Vision, Aspirations & Values," <www.levi strauss.com/about/vision.html>, accessed February 14, 2000.

5. "Dell Vision Mission Statement," <www.dell.com/us/en/gen/corporate/vision_mission.html>, accessed February 14, 2000.

6. Surprisingly, the author has come across a number of large and small companies where this has been the practice.

7. H. Weihrich, "The TOWS Matrix—A Tool for Situational Analysis," *Long Range Planning* 15, no. 2 (1982), pp. 54–66.

8. E. Schonfeld, "Cisco & the Kids: Are They as Scary as They Look?" *Fortune,* April 14, 1997, pp. 200–02.

9. G. Hamel, "Killer Strategies," *Fortune,* June 23, 1997, pp. 70–84.

10. M. E. Porter, *Competitive Advantage Creating and Sustaining Superior Performance* (New York: Free Press, 1985).

11. M. E. Porter and V. E. Millar, "How Information Technology Gives You a Competitive Advantage," *Harvard Business Review,* July–August 1985, pp. 149–60.

12. K. Barron, "Bill Gates Wants Our Business," *Forbes,* April 6, 1998, pp. 46–47.

13. J. F. Rockart, "Chief Executives Define Their Own Data Needs," *Harvard Business Review,* March–April 1979, pp. 81–93.

14. M. E. Porter, *Competitive Advantage Creating and Sustaining Superior Performance* (New York: Free Press, 1985).

15. S. Anderson Forest and D. Weimer, "Cable, Phone, Internet . . . Who Ya Gonna Call?" *Business Week,* March 1, 1999, pp. 64–66.

16. S. Lohr, "Again, It's Microsoft vs. the World," *New York Times,* February 13, 2000, section 3, pp. 1, 16–17.

17. H. Weihrich, "The TOWS Matrix—A Tool for Situational Analysis," *Long Range Planning* 15, no. 2 (1982), pp. 54–66.

18. The originator of the term "SMART" goals/objectives remains unclear.

19. The Balanced Scorecard (see R. Kaplan and D. Norton, *The Balanced Scorecard* [Boston: Harvard Business School Press, 1996]) has become especially popular as a planning tool among senior managers. The Balanced Scorecard advocates four categories of metrics—namely financial, customer, internal business process, and learning and growth—for capturing a company's performance. However, the BI model has two advantages over the Balanced Scorecard. First, the BI model requires a clear definition of business direction, including vision and/or mission, business goals, and strategies. These elements lay the foundation for all subsequent low-level SMART objectives (measures or metrics), strategies, and tools. With the BI model, managers can go beyond Kaplan and Norton's four categories and include all goals, objectives, and strategies that address the critical aspects of their business. Second, by aligning and linking techniques and tools to objectives and strategies, the BI model shows clearly where organizational capabilities are developing, resources are spent, and techniques and tools are applied in all areas of the business. Kaplan and Norton's approach does not link business direction to deployment of specific techniques and tools. Yet this comprehensive linkage—which is provided by the BI model—is exactly what is needed to implement strategies across the business and achieve multiple goals and objectives.

20. The company's business goals are SMART in nature. This is not uncommon for a company that is held by a larger corporation.

CHAPTER 4

Identifying Target Customers and Assessing Their Needs and Expectations

"If we aren't customer-driven, our cars won't be, either."
—Harold "Red" Poling, former CEO, Ford Motor Company

The recent customer backlash against the major airlines demonstrates that the big companies have forgotten what's important to their customers. As a result, emerging carriers are gaining a foothold in a number of markets by offering better services and lower prices.[1] Misunderstanding customer needs is not unique to the airline industry. For example, in Japan, Ford builds a Taurus that is too long for Tokyo parking spaces. It's no wonder that Ford is pulling the plug on the Japanese Taurus and has been in the red for the last two years.[2]

In order for companies to be successful, they have to deliver products and services that consumers need, want, even crave. It's obvious! Yet the business press is replete with stories of lost opportunities. In the 1980s, the major U.S. automakers, namely GM, Ford, and Chrysler, failed to learn these lessons and allowed Japanese imports to gain unprecedented market share as a result. Companies do well when they define their target customers, assess their needs and expectations, and meet or exceed those expectations. To gain an enhanced understanding of customers, a company needs to address three basic questions.

1. Who are our customers?
2. What do they need?
3. How well are their needs being met?

Who Are Our Customers?

Companies cannot operate in every market and satisfy every need. A company that is trying to be everything to everyone is setting itself up for failure. Consequently, a company has to define a group of customers—a target market or market segment—within the whole market of potential buyers who would be interested in its products and services.[3] The target market is composed of people who have similar reactions to a given market mix, which consists of product and service benefits, price, promotion, and place.[4] The company has to serve these customers well and make a profit. For example, Buy.com's market is the extremely cost-conscious who buy over the Web; Gucci focuses on the extremely affluent; and The Limited targets young, fashion-conscious men and women. Companies that define their target customers can focus on exactly the needs that mean the most to those customers. These companies divert their attention away from product characteristics and service activities that are either not wanted or unappreciated.

Generally, companies select segmentation variables, including gender, education level, and income to define a target market (e.g., women with graduate degrees who earn over $80,000 annually). Companies determine the nature and number of variables to be used for defining target markets. Market segmentation benefits companies by

- permiting identification of customers,
- helping companies design products and services to meet customers' needs, and
- allowing companies to develop effective promotions to stimulate demand.

Although segmentation approaches range from no segmentation (serve the whole market) to concentrated segmentation (serve one segment only), most companies serve several segments simultaneously.

Ill-defined and/or large target markets make the process of defining who the customer is extremely tricky. Consider a company selling electronic components for PCs. The customers are both the companies that assemble the PCs and the design engineers who decide on the components that go into the PCs. Each group of customers has different needs. For example, the manufacturers need components in large quantities, timely deliveries, and accurate invoicing. Design engineers require access to specifications, schematics, and a small number of components for prototyping. A company needs to understand each type of customer it services because the customer's needs and wants may be different, as demonstrated previously. Hewlett-Packard (HP) recognizes that its customers fall into two camps: those who want low-cost, no-frills products and services and those who want sophisticated business solutions. The latter group requires HP to analyze business processes, manage projects, and build and install computer-based systems that may incorporate hardware from other suppliers. Being able to provide these services in addition to the hardware is a large part of HP's current success. Marriott also pursues several well-defined groups of customers, as reflected in the company's multiple offerings, including Marriott Hotels, Marriott Extended Stay, and Fairfield Inns, with each type of lodging satisfying the differing requirements of the respective target markets.

Most companies have a good sense of who their customers are, but some don't. When Arthur Martinez became CEO of Sears, he found that the company had no clue as to who the target customer was. To establish focus, he chose the middle-American mom and packed the isles with women's apparel.[5] The company's profits rebounded and Sears reestablished itself as one of America's preeminent retailers. In a number of industries, the 80-20 rule is applicable: 80 percent of the profits come from 20 percent of all customers. Detailed analysis of scanner data at Price Chopper, a large, privately owned grocery chain, clearly demonstrates this rule. Because of the 80-20 phenomenon, the company is in the process of identifying the profitable customers for targeted and well-earned promotions from the less profitable customers, who mainly "cherry pick" specially priced merchandise. The process of separating profitable from less profitable customers is a time-consuming task, but emerging commercially available software makes it easier to perform.

What Do They Need?

Customers want their expectations satisfied or exceeded the first time and every time. Customers' perceptions of unsatisfactory and satisfactory service are a function of their a priori expectations and actual experiences: they're dissatisfied when expectations are not fulfilled by actual experience; satisfied when expectations are fulfilled; and very satisfied, or thrilled, when they are exceeded. Good companies understand their customers' needs and satisfy those needs, whereas great companies draw out and satisfy preemergent needs that customers can't articulate because they're not fully aware of them.

Companies can define target markets, but fail to understand fully the needs of their customers. Understanding customers' needs doesn't take a lot of sophisticated, high-priced, technical market research. Considering the competitive forces (e.g., quality, price, and speed) that drive today's business and recognizing that customers' demands are escalating, it is safe to say that at a base level, customers want the highest quality, at the lowest possible price, as quickly as possible. These are three dimensions that are important to customers in all markets and industries. According to Rob Rodin, CEO of Marshall Industries, a computer and electronics distributor, the customers' imperatives are: "We want it free. We want it perfect. We want it now."[6] These imperatives provide a basis for thinking about what customers need and for suggesting characteristics of products and services that they would want.

Price and speed are relatively straightforward to comprehend. With regard to price, customers want to spend as little as possible. That's not to say customers will not spend more money for higher quality, more convenience, and so on, but all things being equal, most customers are price conscious and act accordingly. Speed is essential in today's world. With development, production, and delivery times constantly shrinking, customers have become accustomed to receiving their products and services quickly, easily, and conveniently. Concerning quality, there is a need to differentiate between product and service quality. Product quality involves the tangible aspects of any product or service. For example, with a financial services company, the financial statement represents one tangible aspect of the service. It should be 100 percent error-free to contribute to high levels of product quality. Service quality encompasses the less tangible aspects of a service, characteristics that are experienced by customers. With a financial services company, the considerable experience of a financial advisor is one aspect of service quality. It imparts a sense of competency to a customer. Product quality is about what's delivered, whereas service quality is about how it's delivered. The basic dimensions of product quality are

- performance—the product's primary operating characteristics;
- features—characteristics that supplement the product's operating characteristics;

- reliability—probability that a product will operate correctly for a period of time;
- conformance (to specifications)—degree to which the product fulfills stipulated design specifications;
- durability—operating life of the product;
- serviceability—ease of servicing the product;
- aesthetics—a (subjective) measure of how the product looks, feels, smells, and so on; and
- perceived quality—overall quality reputation of the company.[7]

Companies don't have to compete on all dimensions equally, only the ones that are pertinent to their target customers. For example, Porsche builds high-performance cars (performance) that can be driven hard often (reliability) and, with reasonable maintenance, will last a long time (durability), because these are the primary reasons (excluding image) why Porsche enthusiasts buy the company's cars. In designing the Malibu for the midsize market, GM's design team specified a hierarchy of characteristics: the pyramid started with dependability, reliability, and safety at the base, specified the most important considerations of customers, and ranked twenty-eight elements, ending with storage space, entertainment systems, and interior lighting.[8] Clearly, GM is emphasizing only a subset of the available dimensions of product quality, focusing on only those dimensions that are most meaningful to its customers.

There are several dimensions of service quality that can augment the product quality characteristics. These dimensions are

- reliability—consistency of performance (i.e., the correct service, the first time, and every time);
- responsiveness—willingness to provide service or timeliness of service;
- access—ease of access and waiting time;
- competency—skills and knowledge for providing service;
- courtesy—degree of politeness, civility, and friendliness of contact personnel;
- communication—ability to keep customers informed, listening to customers, and explaining the service;
- credibility—trustworthiness and honesty;
- security—freedom from harm or risk;

- understanding—ability to understand customers' needs and recognize regular customers; and
- tangibles—physical facilities, appearance of contact personnel, and physical representation of service.[9]

When customers can't perceive differences between like products, the determinants of service quality become especially important. As innovation cycles shrink—turning products into commodities—bundling the dimensions of service quality with products may become the only way of competing successfully. GE Power Generation and GE Capital were first to recognize that the product itself was sometimes less important than the financing of it. By discovering that financing was an important service, GE was able to modify its sales, quoting, and financing processes before its competitors (Siemens and ABB), outdistancing them in the marketplace. Consider the PC industry. As prices decline (e.g., Microworkz Computer Corporation will begin selling PCs for just $299)[10] and the basic components of computers become the same, to keep its sales up Dell Computer lets customers configure their own PCs online and track assembly and shipping status. Although these services aren't the only reasons for the company's success, they are important contributing factors. Dell also has stellar manufacturing and logistics competencies, which allow the company to offer competitive prices. As with the dimensions of product quality, companies need to understand which service quality factors are right for their customers.

Companies can define each dimension of product and service quality in concrete terms and rank them according to their relative importance to customers. Capital Carpet, a company that advises on, orders, and installs flooring materials, delineates the determinants of product and service quality that are most important to the customers of its four target markets: individual consumers, contractors, property managers, and designers. The dimensions of service quality include provision of product specifications (competence), storage facilities (tangibles), and transportation of materials to job sites in a timely manner (responsiveness) (see Table 4.1). Moreover, depending on the target market, some factors are more important than others. For example, provision of on-time deliveries, as determined by the construction schedule, is the most important factor for contractors, whereas assisting in the development of specifications and provision of price estimates are the most important factors for individual consumers (see Table 4.2).

TABLE 4.1

Characteristics of Service and Product Quality at Capital Carpet

General Dimensions	Specific Characteristics	Service Quality Dimensions	Product Quality Dimensions
Product specifications	Provide price and durability information, product specifications, and installation advice	Reliability Competence	
Support materials	Provide flooring-specific installation materials (not always readily available to the customer)		Conformance
Receiving	Provide capability to handle large and unwieldy materials	Responsiveness Accessibility	
Materials preparation	Prepare flooring and provide off-gassing service	Responsiveness Accessibility Competence Security	
Materials storage	Provide storage for all materials	Responsiveness Accessibility	
Delivery	Transport all materials to installation area	Responsiveness Accessibility	
Installation	Remove old flooring, install new flooring, and dispose of all materials	Responsiveness Accessibility Competence	

TABLE 4.2
Specific Characteristics for Capital Carpet's Target Markets

Target Markets	Specific Characteristics
Individual consumer	Provide price and durability information and product specifications Provide capability to handle large and unwieldy materials Provide flooring-specific installation materials Prepare flooring and provide off-gassing service
Contractor	Provide capability to handle large and unwieldy materials Transport all materials to installation area Provide reliable workforce for installation
Property management	Provide professional business approach Transport all materials to installation area Provide reliable workforce for installation
Designer	Provide professional business approach Provide price and durability information and product specifications Provide space and calculation services

If a company hits upon the optimal combination of product and service factors and price, it shouldn't become too comfortable. Customer needs, expectations, and their relative importance change over time. There are two primary reasons for this.

1. Today's customers may not be tomorrow's customers, because the needs and expectations of the target market change.
2. What's new today becomes old tomorrow as customers become acclimated to higher levels of performance introduced by competitors and new products and services.

The changing demographics and psychometrics of a target market constantly challenge companies to keep up. Nordstrom, the most admired department store retailer of the early 1990s, may be losing touch with some of its customers' needs. Although working women moved to more casual attire for the office, Nordstrom continued to stock its old, buttoned-down styles, turning a number of customers off and depressing earnings.[11] In designing the new Malibu, GM was surprised to learn many buyers in the mid-size market no longer viewed a car as a means of personal expression. The company found that people considered cars as tools and gave the highest priority to reliability and durability in selecting cars.[12]

The dimensions of product and service quality expected by customers form a progressive hierarchy of three performance levels: base, stated or customer-specified, and preemergent.[13] Base expectations or levels of performance are unstated, because customers assume their presence; if a company fails to meet these expectations, customers are dissatisfied. Airline passengers never think about asking for dinner on transatlantic flights because all large commercial carriers provide it. Stated, or customer-specified, performance expectations are articulated during the course of making a purchase decision. When buying a new car, a shopper might specify his or her need for air conditioning, leather interior, and a five-speed transmission. Preemergent expectations are not articulated by customers (and often go undiscovered for some time by the companies that serve them). When these expectations are fulfilled, customers are highly satisfied with a company's performance. Smart-thinking companies deliver both the base and customer-specified expectations. Additionally, they discover preemergent characteristics and act on them before their competitors, delighting customers and building loyalty along the way.

Companies create real value breakthroughs, or innovations, by insisting that managers discover the preemergent ways of satisfying and winning customers. In addition to understanding customers' base and stated needs and expectations, these companies create need, giving customers the ability to do something they never thought of doing before. They initiate new technology cycles, industry standards, and business rules. As a result, these companies often leapfrog the competition, breaking the cycle of competitive benchmarking and incremental innovation (even imitation) that ensues. Sony is legendary for attempting to lead its customers with new products and services rather than asking customers what they want. As a result, Sony developed the Walkman, even though market research indicated that few people would buy it. The company deemphasizes market research in favor of refined thinking about a product's use, trying to derive characteristics that customers don't know they want at present.[14] Silicon Graphics Incorporated (SGI) cultivates the customers that are most difficult to satisfy. These are customers who want to perform activities that can't be accomplished with existing products. SGI works with these customers to satisfy their dreams and unmet demands. This approach often provides the energy for designing the next generation of SGI technology.[15]

Expectations in the hierarchy migrate downward over time because of competitors' actions, new process innovations, and new applications of information technology. Toyota went to great lengths to delight customers when it introduced the Lexus automobile and its service package. The first two maintenance visits were free, the cars were detailed, and customer drop-offs at and pick ups from work were standard practice. This approach to service delighted customers and forced competitors to follow suit. Today, these service attributes constitute an important part of an upscale dealership's overall service package. The basic expectations of mass merchandisers (e.g., Wal-Mart, Kmart, and Target) include over 98 percent fill rates, on-time deliveries, and short lead-times. Specified requirements include customer-specific case packs, placement of bar codes, and store-ready packaging. Suppliers that satisfy these requirements are operating at best-practice levels. As supplier-retailer logistics systems become leaner and more reliant on operations data, the preemergent expectations of mass merchandisers will include data integrity and accuracy. What's exciting today will become a base expectation or minimally accepted level of performance over time as best practices become industrywide, standard operating procedures.

The prevailing wisdom suggests that misspecification of a product's or service's characteristics can be costly. Offering too little (an inferior combination of product and service benefits at low performance levels) could result in lost sales, yet offering too much (profusion of product and service benefits at higher than required performance levels) could hurt profit margins (see Figure 4.1). Companies must strike the correct balance to continually please customers and earn high returns.

FIGURE 4.1
Specification of Service Offerings

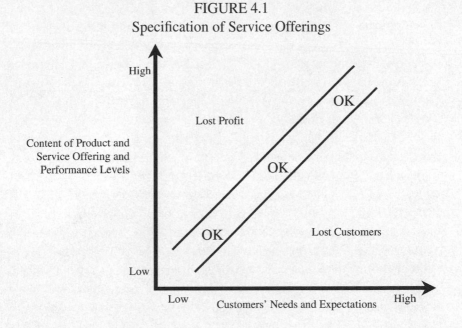

How Well Are Their Needs Being Met?

Great companies develop a solid understanding of their customers' needs and expectations and continually monitor their performance to ensure that customers are not disappointed. They use new insights about customers and shortcomings in operating systems performance to make improvements in their offerings and correct deficiencies, respectively. There are a number of approaches for developing an understanding of customer needs and expectations and for measuring the degree to which a company satisfies its customers. These approaches form an information-content continuum for understanding customer expectations and measuring customer satisfaction (see Figure 4.2). Low-content approaches include unsolicited, unrecorded complaints and benchmarking, which provide little information about customers' expectations. High-content approaches include formal surveys, focus groups, and customer interviews. These approaches are capable of capturing important needs and measuring customer satisfaction directly. A company should use as many approaches as possible.

FIGURE 4.2

Information Content of Approaches for Understanding Customers

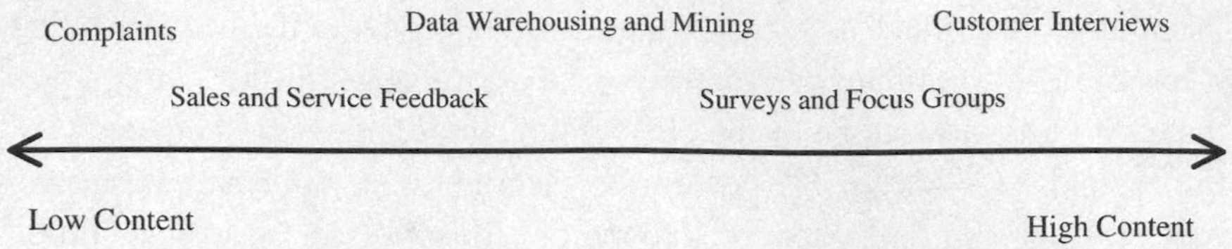

Complaints   Data Warehousing and Mining   Customer Interviews

Sales and Service Feedback   Surveys and Focus Groups

←——→

Low Content   High Content

Many companies believe that they can learn a lot from complaints. The nature of the data and the lack of systems designed to exploit complaints limit their overall usefulness. Complaints emerge from a highly biased group of customers who are so dissatisfied that they take the time to register a complaint. Generally, they focus on only those product and service characteristics to which they attribute their dissatisfaction. In many companies, personnel either dismiss complaints outright or become overly defensive. Some companies log complaints into manual or computer systems to be examined at a later time. However, the format of the data precludes the development of systems for easy manipulation in order to discover meaningful insights, trends, and relationships to affecting physical processes. Yet complaints do impart some information about the existence of dissatisfied customers and the potential reasons or causes of their dissatisfaction. Well-run companies heed complaints and develop internal systems and procedures for processing them.

Benchmarking competitors is another way to learn about customers. Knowing who their customers are and how they serve them provides valuable insight. Before entering new markets, the executives of Cracker Barrel, a large restaurant chain, embark on eating frenzies—visits to local family restaurants, eating as much as ten meals a day—to discover what passes as "authentic" cooking in those markets. The managers reproduce local favorites (for example, Reuben sandwich platters in upstate New York) so as not to disappoint its customers. Many of the company's customers are loyal, repeat customers who are traveling and enjoy Cracker Barrel's home cooking. Cracker Barrel earns twice as much as competitors Bob Evans Farms, Shoneys, and Coco's.[16]

Sales and service personnel communicate directly with customers and are an alternate source of information about customer needs. Sales personnel are responsible for moving product, and service associates for providing service (e.g., answering product or service-related questions). Generally, listening to customers' expectations, gathering data about them, and feeding it back to their company are not their primary responsibilities. Companies that don't take advantage of the close interaction that occurs between customers and sales and service personnel to learn more about customer needs, expectations, and customer satisfaction are forsaking an important source of information. A number of companies have systems in place to minimize the effort associated with gathering and analyzing the data available through these conduits.

Data warehousing and data mining are complementary approaches for organizing and analyzing large amounts of transaction data about customers. The data warehouse (or scaled-down and highly focused data mart) provides an environment for deploying decision support and data mining applications, which shed light on customers' purchasing behavior, including needs, preferences, and buying patterns. These applications can define customers' complementary needs for products and services, relationships between personal characteristics and consumer behavior, and relationships between events over time. Some companies use these applications to determine which customers would most benefit from a specific promotion, thus maximizing customer satisfaction. The proliferation of applications, especially in retailing, financial services, and health care, has forced many companies in these industries to adopt data warehousing and mining as an additional means to learn more about customer needs and expectations.

Focus groups, formal surveys, and customer interviews are the best ways for understanding customers' needs and expectations and for measuring customer satisfaction, because they can be specifically designed to extract this information from customers. ScrubaDub, a family-owned chain of car washes, after examining customer survey data, redesigned its business to provide exactly what its target customers wanted: personalized service, guarantees, and an attractive environment. The company has grown to become one of the top twenty car wash operations in the United States.[17] Many companies are moving to the Internet to collect customer data. For example, Hyundai Motor America, a maker of small and midsize autos, uses an online customer satisfaction survey to see how well it is doing. To encourage customers to respond to the questionnaire, the company offers a

$500 coupon that customers can apply against the price of a new auto. According to Paul Epstein, manager of interactive communication, "When we finish our survey, we will have a comprehensive information base and be able to staff up newer services."[18]

There is often concern over the ability to measure the dimensions of service quality, including courtesy, competence, and credibility, because they are intangible. However, five-point rating scales and Likert scales allow companies to handle issues related to these characteristics easily. For example, the following question can be used as part of a questionnaire to measure customer satisfaction: "Considering everything, how satisfied are you with our service?" with Very Dissatisfied = 1, Dissatisfied = 2, Neither = 3, Satisfied = 4, and Very Satisfied = 5. Focus groups and customer interviews can offer insights that can't be captured with a survey because they are less structured in nature, allowing participants to delve into promising areas as they see fit.

All of these approaches are information-gathering activities that rely on listening to customers, examining their survey responses, or analyzing their purchasing behavior. Some companies go beyond these traditional approaches, seeking to understand their customers better than they understand themselves. For example, the calculator division of Texas Instruments (TI) sends managers to work with mathematics teachers to learn how they integrate calculations into their teaching. The managers also simulate classrooms to better understand how students and teachers interact with one another and how improved calculators help them in the classroom.[19] In a less expensive approach, Tom Kasten, a vice president with Levi Strauss who is responsible for developing products for American teenagers, would visit the Fillmore Auditorium on a weekly basis to talk to kids about what they were looking for in a pair of jeans and to observe how they customized them. This extra duty allowed him to observe Levi's customers in their natural habitats and learn about those product and service characteristics that matter most and delight customers.[20]

Regardless of the approaches used, companies have to feed everything they learn, infer, or deduce about customers back into themselves, including who their customers are, what their needs and expectations are, and how the company is performing in terms of satisfying or exceeding those needs and expectations. Once a company brings this type of information in-house, the pressure is on to produce products and services that satisfy or exceed customers' needs and expectations. Good companies have processes and procedures for making sure that functional areas know what existing and potential customers may be thinking about at any moment and how they're performing vis-à-vis existing customers' expectations.

Learning about Customers at Reader's Digest

Reader's Digest–U.S.A., a publisher of a popular magazine of the same name and producer of do-it-yourself books, videos, and music products, uses several methods over time for staying in touch with customers and monitoring customer satisfaction. The company's customer service department and its suppliers are in direct contact (e.g., phone) and indirect contact (e.g., mail) with customers and perform a number of functions, including handling inquiries, logging and resolving complaints, processing notifications (for instance, change of address), and processing orders. The department categorizes every complaint into major types of complaints, including price, policies, operations, and magazine (for example, editorial). Additionally, the department periodically distributes a short customer satisfaction survey to a sample of customers who recently contacted the department. The questionnaire contains several questions and directives, including:

- How satisfied are you with the level of service provided by Reader's Digest in response to your needs?
- Please indicate your satisfaction with how we responded to your written correspondence request.
- Based on your experience, how likely is it that you will continue to purchase Reader's Digest products?

Respondents use scales that range from "very dissatisfied" to "very satisfied" (for the first two items) and "definitely" to "definitely not" (for the last item). Reader's Digest uses the survey data to determine if problems persist after the company has taken corrective action. Additionally, every three years, Reader's Digest conducts a large-scale customer expectation survey. This survey is comprehensive and covers product and service characteristics, including

- ordering and service preferences,
- value of an 800 number, and
- effectiveness of product distribution.

Each month the department produces several reports, including a complaint report for its vice president, who shares the reports with other divisional vice presidents. The reports provide managers with useful data about products, services, complaints, and customer satisfaction, which helps them understand how to deliver greater value to their customers.

Management Directives

There are several lessons that can be derived from the previous examples:

- Think from the outside in. Customers determine what's important. They define the relevant characteristics of the products and services that companies offer and the appropriate level of performance. Using many of the data capture and analysis techniques (for example, focus groups, interviews, and surveys) previously described, companies can uncover base and user-specified needs and expectations that they need to satisfy in order to be successful. This process leads to incremental, or market-driven, improvements in products and services. In many cases, product and service failures occur because companies neglect to put customers first, satisfy their expectations, and make requisite changes to their products and services.
- Realize that customers' expectations are dynamic. Customers' needs and expectations are constantly changing. Companies have to constantly make adjustments to accommodate their customers' changing lifestyles, life stages, tastes, and preferences. Additionally, competitors are constantly raising the bar by introducing new combinations of product quality, service quality, and price. The net result is that customers' expectations are continually ratcheting upward with no end in sight. The rate of change is especially troubling. Web-based businesses are introducing new busi-

ness models that elevate customer satisfaction levels. For example, Amazon.com has improved the process of buying books and CDs with its online reviews, low prices, and convenient home delivery.

- Think from the inside out. Companies that encourage innovative thinking can discover innovative ways to satisfy customers. These companies not only ask their customers what they want, but also create and incorporate innovative product and service characteristics into their offerings. Companies can challenge customers' assumptions and consider potential needs that haven't been met. By planning to lead customers rather than be led by them, they satisfy preemergent expectations, amazing their customers and earning the admiration (and jealousy) of their competitors. This process results in technologically superior products and services that often change the nature of competition.

- Capture expectations and performance as actionable information. The data capture and analysis techniques can help companies translate needs and expectations into actionable information so that companies never miss the target and are in tune with potentially emerging trends. Moreover, they help companies understand how well they are doing in the eyes of the customer. Companies have to institute systems for continually capturing customer needs and expectations and for assessing how well it is satisfying those needs and expectations.

Notes

1. W. Zellner, "Straightened Up and Flying Right," *Business Week,* April 5, 1999, pp. 40, 42.

2. K. Naughton, E. Thornton, and P. Magnusson, "A Car Wreck of a Car Strategy," *Business Week,* April 19, 1999, pp. 40, 42.

3. T. Levitt, *Management for Business Growth* (New York: McGraw-Hill, 1969). The term "target market" is synonymous with the term "market segment." The former is preferred here to emphasize the need for companies to target a group of customers within a larger market.

4. Here, the product component of the traditional marketing mix (i.e., product, price, promotion, and place) consists of both product and service dimensions.

5. P. Sellers, "Sears: The Turnaround Is Ending; The Revolution Has Begun," *Fortune,* April 28, 1997, pp. 106, 108, 110, 114, 116, 118.

6. P. Hood, "Who's the Boss?" *New Media,* October 1998, pp. 30–37.

7. D. A. Garvin, "Competing on the Eight Dimensions of Quality," *Harvard Business Review,* November–December 1987, pp. 101–09.

8. R. Blumenstein, "Struggle to Remake the Malibu Says a Lot about Remaking GM," *Wall Street Journal,* March 27, 1997, pp. A1, A8.

9. L. Berry, V. Zeithamal, and P. Parasuraman, "Quality Counts in Service Too," *Business Horizons* 28, no. 3 (1985), pp. 44–52.

10. P. Burrows and I. Sager, "PC Makers Think beyond the Box," *Business Week,* April 19, 1999, pp. 148–50.

11. S. Browder, "Great Service Wasn't Enough," *Business Week,* April 19, 1999, pp. 126–27.

12. R. Blumenstein, "Struggle to Remake the Malibu Says a Lot about Remaking GM," *Wall Street Journal,* March 27, 1997, pp. A1, A8.

13. A. Tenner and I. J. DeToro, *Total Quality Management* (Reading, MA: Addison-Wesley, 1992).

14. G. Hamel and C. K. Prahalad, "Seeing the Future First," *Fortune,* September 5, 1994, pp. 64–70.

15. A. Deutschman, "The Managing Wisdom of High-Tech Superstars," *Fortune,* October 17, 1994, pp. 197–203.

16. A. J. Tarquinio, "King of Grits Alters Menu to Reflect Northern Tastes," *Wall Street Journal,* September 22, 1997, pp. B1, B5.

17. D. McDougall, "Know Thy Customer," *Wall Street Journal,* August 7, 1995, p. A12.

18. K. Chin Leong, "Customer Service Gets Royal Treatment," *Internet Week,* September 14, 1998, p. 32.

19. M. Hammer and S. A. Stanton, "The Power of Reflection," *Fortune,* November 24, 1997, pp. 291–96.

20. Ibid.

CHAPTER 5

Defining a Value Proposition

"When you buy a Lexus, you don't buy a product. You buy a luxury package."

—George Borst, former General Manager, Lexus

Delivering real value to customers should be a company's most important objective. Economic value added, growth, and other performance measures are byproducts of delivering customer value. Customers make purchasing decisions based on perceived value, or the degree to which their needs and expectations about product quality, service quality, and/or price are satisfied. With an understanding of its mission, goals, and strategies and of its customers' needs and expectations, a company can develop a value proposition for delivering superior value to its customers that will allow it to attract new customers, retain existing customers, and deliver significant profits. If a company maximizes value for its customers, success follows. In fact, the keys to success in today's business world are

- ability to understand what constitutes value in the minds of customers and
- ability to continually deliver that value better than the competition.

The former directive is (generally speaking) a marketing challenge. Companies need a good and sustainable value proposition for their customers. David Morrison, a management consultant, says it succinctly: "One thing you can count on . . . if you don't create a better deal for your customer, somebody else will."[1] The latter directive is a challenge for the business functions, employees, partners, and subcontractors involved with the delivery of the product or service. Robert Herres, CEO of USAA, an insurance and financial services company, summarizes these viewpoints in three sentences. "First you decide who you want your customers to be. Then you decide what they need and want. Then you figure out which of those needs you can meet, and then you do that better than anyone else."[2]

Concerning a value proposition, as a caveat, companies need to be careful that beating the competition doesn't become the overriding concern. It may lead to incremental improvements in value innovation (i.e., just ahead of the competition) rather than real-value innovations or breakthroughs. By emphasizing the delivery of value to customers and by striving to create value breakthroughs via product, service, and/or price superiority, companies place the customer at the center of their thinking and challenge employees to change the nature of the game in their industries. For example, GE encourages managers to develop "game changers": new products, services, business processes, technologies, and so forth that create value for their customers and economic value for themselves. The innovations may augment existing products and services or may lead to completely new business opportunities for the company. For example, Vendor Managed Inventory (VMI) is a new GE Plastics business that collects data from various points in the supply chain. Using sophisticated algorithms, the company provides suppliers and customers with information that helps smooth variations in ordering, inventory, and shipping and that optimizes critical resources, such as capacity, energy, inventory, and labor. Value chain participants never asked for VMI's services but are sure glad they have them now.

Dimensions of Value

The basic ingredients of customer value are product quality, service quality, and price. Together they form the Value Cube (see Figure 5.1). The cube suggests that companies can increase value by meeting or exceeding customers' expectations along any one, or all, of these dimensions. Companies deliver innovative, or breakthrough, customer value when they make a quantum leap along all three dimensions simultaneously. Recent problems at Compaq demonstrate the value of all three value dimensions. The company's strengths (i.e., high-quality computers and a great brand name) are inadequate in today's market. Corporations now demand more than just quality products; they also want low prices and support for their machines

FIGURE 5.1
Customer Value Cube

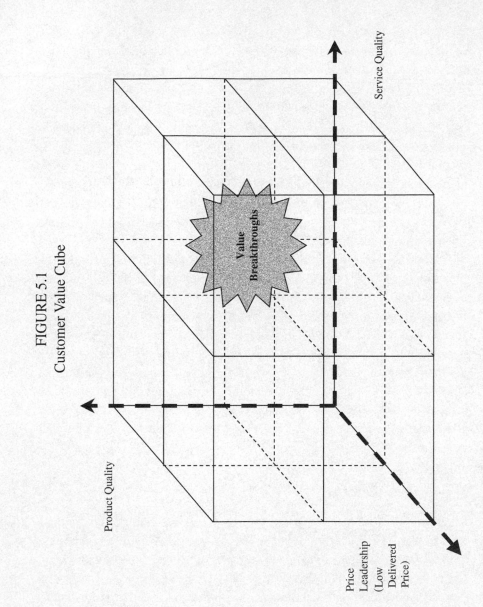

Service Quality

Product Quality

Price
Leadership
(Low
Delivered
Price)

Value
Breakthroughs

83

and networks. In response, Compaq is examining ways, including the acquisition of companies, to quickly develop the service quality and price dimensions of the Value Cube.[3]

The Value Cube applies to every type of business. Product-producing companies make physical, tangible products, can inventory their output, have generally low customer contact, and are capital-intensive (see Table 5.1). On the other hand, service-producing companies offer intangible products, cannot inventory their output, have high customer contact, and are labor-intensive. The classic distinctions between these types of companies are fading because every product is associated with some service and every service has a tangible component. For example, the delivery and installation of a refrigerator includes delivery during a certain time window (e.g., between 3:00 P.M. and 5:00 P.M.), descriptions of operation and maintenance procedures, and a high amount of customer contact. Similarly, the bill that follows a visit to a physician's office is a tangible item (hopefully, free of errors) that can be inventoried and involves little customer contact during its preparation.

A company's value proposition is a strategy about how it expects to deliver value to customers along the Value Cube's various dimensions. From

TABLE 5.1
Classic Distinctions between Product-
and Service-Producing Companies

Product-Producing Companies	*Service-Producing Companies*
Tangible output	Intangible output
Output can be inventoried	Output cannot be inventoried
Customer is absent	Customer is present (and may be a participant)
Site selection may be independent of customers	Site selection is dictated by customers
Scale economics	Limited scale economics
Capital-intensive	Labor-intensive
Measurable output	Difficult to measure output

another angle, companies can define customer value as product quality plus service quality divided by price:

$$\text{Customer Value} = \frac{\text{Product Quality} + \text{Service Quality}}{\text{Price}}$$

(This equation portrays the concept of customer value only; as a result, it doesn't reduce customer value to a scalar quantity.) The determinants of product quality include performance, features, and reliability, whereas the determinants of service quality include responsiveness, access, and competency. Thus value is a bundle, or aggregation, of product and service benefits for a price. Companies that offer a unique value proposition will be successful. Companies can increase value using one or more of the following strategies:

- Decrease the denominator by reducing prices, leaving product and/or service benefits constant.
- Enlarge the numerator by increasing any of the product and/or service benefits, leaving prices constant.
- Do both: improve the product and/or service benefits and lower prices simultaneously.

Successful companies offer an imaginative combination of various product and service benefits at prices that win and retain customers. The "best," or most successful, companies offer radically superior value that's based upon quantum leaps in product and service quality at the lowest prices. Drew Nieporent, the proprietor of seven restaurants, embodies this strategy through his winning formula, which is: consistently good food (product quality) in lovely settings (service quality) at reasonable, even bargain, prices.[4]

The Low-Price Approach to Value

Companies that deploy the first strategy listed above can be successful as long as customers perceive value in their product or service offerings. These companies attempt to beat everyone all of the time on price, imparting the perception of an exceptional deal. Ross Stores, a seller of "packaway" apparel and merchandise (end-of-season goods that fail to sell when in season), hangs its apparel on racks by size and type to help customers quickly identify merchandise and reduce browsing time. However, Ross Stores does not provide attentive service. According to one marketing consultant, careless service "is the price you pay for the discount. It's worth it."[5] Management points out that "Customers are coming in for a bargain, if not necessarily for a blouse."[6] In recent years, the company's rapid growth and profitability demonstrate that customers perceive Ross Stores as providing significant value.

Buy.com aims to offer the lowest prices on all their merchandise. The company is totally committed to being the price leader in a number of product categories, even if this means losing money on some sales. Specialized software searches competitors' sites for the lowest prices. If it's not the lowest, Buy.com undercuts the price and sends it to price-comparing search engines that make it available to customers almost immediately. The company's revenues are tied to advertising collected from the manufacturers that sell through its Web site. Despite being the lowest-price Web site for the merchandise it sells, the company comes up short on customer service, ease of use, and overall customer experience relative to its competitors (e.g., Amazon.com).[7]

The Product and Service Quality Approach to Value

Despite the success of the low-price approach, in most industries the trend is to move away from price-based competition by expanding the bundle of product and service benefits, offering greater value to customers (even at prices above what the competition charges), and deriving greater margins in the process. At GE's lighting business, according to one executive, price competition is not a core value of the company.[8]

The trend is especially apparent in the gasoline retailing business. Mobile Corporation is emphasizing a variety of services at their gas stations, from cappuccino in the convenience stores to helpful attendants at the pumps. The company's data on two thousand motorists reveals that only 20 percent of them purchase gasoline based on price per se. Road warriors (higher-income, middle-aged men who drive between twenty-five thousand and fifty thousand miles per year) and true blues (men and women who are loyal to a brand and even particular stations), who represent about a third of all customers, want a variety of services. These services include classier snacks; human contact; quality products; top-notch, speedy service; and attendants who recognize them.[9] A Mobile executive indicates that "the focus is no longer pricing competition," but "to blow the customer away with product quality and service."[10] The company will keep its gasoline prices reasonably competitive because it believes that motorists will abandon discounters in favor of a "quality buying experience."[11] The new service-oriented strategy is primarily responsible for revenue gains of over 20 percent at stations experimenting with the service concept. Mobil's actions have spurred other companies to take similar steps. For example, to make the process of filling a tank more convenient, Shell is experimenting with a robotic arm, called the "Smart Pump," for automatic fill-ups and with home delivery, where the car is serviced while it sits in the driveway.[12]

Companies that employ the second strategy offer exceptional product and/or service quality. The remarkable success of Papa John's Pizza demonstrates that product quality alone can separate a company from its rivals. The pizza costs more than Little Caesar's and arrives no quicker than Domino's. Moreover, the company offers none of the extra items and amenities found at Pizza Hut, including salads, sandwiches, and restaurant service. For Papa John's, the key to success is the pizza: it is rated as the best-tasting pizza in the markets it serves. Papa John's doesn't attempt to compete on the basis of convenience, variety, and low price; it just wants to have the best-tasting pizza. The company's slogan is "better ingredients, better pizza," and its ingredients include vine-ripened tomatoes, premium mozzarella cheese, and dough prepared with only purified water.[13]

Other companies strongly emphasize service quality. MarineMax, a confederation of boat dealerships, combines high, no-haggle sticker prices with exceptional service. At one of the company's forty-four outlets, a customer could pay about $78,000 for a fully loaded Sea Ray that would cost between $72,000 and $80,000 at competing dealerships. In return for a higher price, the company provides the following:

- a captain who will stay free of charge until the owner learns how to use the boat;
- 24-hour, on-call technicians who can quickly repair a problem that would sink a Sunday outing with the family or, for owners outside of the service area, arrangements with other marinas to provide technical assistance; and
- comprehensive, two-year guarantees for all boats over twenty feet that cover maintenance and service costs.[14]

To cover the costs of these services, MarineMax adds 2.5–6 percent to a boat's purchase price.

To keep customers happy and in a position to purchase a larger boat, MarineMax invites spouses and kids to the marina to learn how to handle their boats and sponsors a variety of "getaways" on regional lakes and exotic locations (e.g., Bahamas). Customers cover the costs, while the company organizes the trips, services the boats, and dispatches technicians and salespersons to accompany the boaters. In an industry where service is abysmal, this service-intensive, value-oriented strategy provides Marine-Max with a competitive edge. The company's pretax profit margin is a little over 7 percent, versus the industry average of 3 percent.[15]

Some companies assume that *just* a lower price, or *just* higher product quality, or *just* higher service quality, is value. As the previous examples demonstrate, they may be correct. However, these companies should continually test these assumptions to ensure their correctness over time because competitors don't stand still and customers' needs and expectations will change.

For example, in the 1980s and early 1990s, compared with U.S. competitors, Japanese companies delivered higher-quality products in a number of industries, including autos, electronics, and semiconductors, thereby imparting higher value to their products. Today, parity exists in many of these industries as U.S. companies have closed the quality gap by implementing quality improvement programs. In many such industries, quality is assumed and the battle is being fought on other grounds, such as service quality and price.

Product Quality, Service Quality, and Low-Price Approach to Value: Creating Value Innovations

Competition makes all products and services like commodities over time. Prices deteriorate and product quality alone fails to differentiate. For example, through e-commerce hubs and software agents, customers can access the lowest prices for comparable products and services. At Imxexchange.com, an online marketplace for mortgage brokers to find loans, brokers place requests for loans and lenders bid on them.[16] In a world like this, prices decline in a hurry.

To be safe, companies should deploy the third strategy, offering innovative combinations of product and service benefits and price. The winning combinations emerge from an accurate assessment of a target market's needs and expectations (outside-in approach), and/or from managers who consider totally new ways of doing things that add value to customers (inside-out approach). Innovative combinations of product quality, service quality, and price are responsible for the highly profitable growth of a number of exemplar companies, including Starbucks, Home Depot, and Intuit.

Kohl's, a Midwest-based chain of department stores, has an innovative, winning combination of product and service benefits and price. The company combines the competitive prices of a mass merchandiser (e.g., Wal-Mart), the appealing shopping experience of Sears or Dillard's, and brand-name merchandise, an approach that goes against conventional retailing wisdom. According to one analyst, "The magic of the company is that it combines the cost structure of a discounter and the brands of a department store."[17] Management stocks the stores with value-priced, brand-name, staple merchandise, including Lee jeans, Fieldcrest sheets, and Reebok shoes. This appeals to its target market, women between the ages of thirty and fifty who have families, a job, and a household income between $20,000 and $70,000 a year. The mix of merchandise is perfectly suited to its shoppers. Recognizing the need to offer convenience and a positive shopping experience, the company provides

- correctly sized, clean, bright stores with a straightforward presentation (all women's merchandise—underwear, blouses, and so on—is grouped together);
- personnel who are encouraged to provide friendly treatment;
- ability to get in and out quickly (whenever two or more customers are queued, sales associates open new registers);
- special amenities, such as baby changing stations and strollers that convert to shopping carts; and
- high in-stock inventory positions.

Analysts praise the company's attention to friendly and pertinent service. Concerning price, Kohl's emphasizes regular and broad promotional sales, making sale prices the everyday prices and keeping the company's

average price lower than the competition for many items. According to
John Herma, COO, "We do twenty simple things that have impact when
taken together. The key is consistency of execution."[18]

Information technology allows companies to make service breakthroughs that customers could never have dreamed possible. The ability to
leverage information and knowledge promotes innovative development
along multiple service dimensions, including responsiveness, access, and
competency. Neoforma.com, a recent Web-based venture, is making it easier for hospital buyers to purchase furnishings and equipment as well as out-
fit entire rooms. Locating and purchasing the items for a new room can take
up to six months, but the Web site can reduce the time by as much as two-
thirds. The site provides an online catalogue of supplies and allows purchasing agents to search by product and type of room. Agents can view floor
plans and individual rooms at a leading hospital and examine lists of items
that belong in a room to gain an understanding of how best to equip and organize a room's contents. They can click on individual products to view detailed pictures, descriptions, and prices from a variety of manufacturers
with links to their Web sites. According to Jeff Kleck, CEO, suppliers "are
getting sales leads from customers they did not even know existed," and,
through the site, hospitals will be able to buy many of the products listed.
The Web site offers twenty-four-hour access and immediate response to an
enormous catalogue (about 1.5 million products) of highly accurate information on rooms and their associated furnishings and equipment.[19]

Management Directives

There are several lessons from the current definition of value that can be
learned from the prior examples.

- Delivering customer value is the key to success. Companies need to understand that customer value is what sells. By striving to offer customers superior value, they can realize highly profitable growth even in aggressively
  competitive markets, as a number of companies that follow this approach
  have demonstrated, including Dell, GE, and Home Depot.
- Devise the winning combination. A winning combination of product
  and service benefits and price exists. Find it! Given an understanding of

its business direction, customers, and their needs and expectations, a company decides on the exact combination of factors. Is it higher product quality? Higher service quality? Lower prices? Or is it time for a major breakthrough? Some companies may have to confront the traditional means of doing business and approach value improvement from the inside out. What characteristics of the products and services can be raised well beyond acceptable standards? What characteristics of the products and services would customers want, even though they don't know it yet? What changes in process and systems design can reduce overall costs so that prices can be lowered? By continually asking these questions and challenging old assumptions, companies can develop a winning combination of product quality, service quality, and/or price.

- Involve the whole organization. The delivery of customer value has implications for an entire organization. It's not just a matter of the ingredients; it is the execution as well. Companies should dream up services that will win customers and then build systems that will deliver those services. All members of the supply chain and distribution channel affect product quality, service quality, and the elements that determine price. The delivery of value involves computer systems, processes, quality procedures, and people.

Notes

1. "Why Baseball Is in Trouble, How GE Makes Money, and Other Insights into the True Origin of Corporate Profits," *Fortune,* May 11, 1998, p. 184.

2. R. Henkoff, "Growing Your Company: Five Ways to Do It Right!" *Fortune,* November 25, 1996, pp. 78–82.

3. D. Kirkpatrick, "Houston, We Have Some Problems," *Fortune,* June 23, 1997, p. 102.

4. J. Vitullo-Martin, "How a Hot Business Keeps Its Sizzle," *Wall Street Journal,* March 24, 1997, p. A18.

5. G. Lau, "Know Thy Customer," *Forbes,* July 7, 1997, p. 76.

6. Ibid.

7. L. Armstrong, "Anything You Sell, I Can Sell Cheaper," *Business Week,* December 14, 1998, pp. 130–32.

8. T. A. Stewart, "Why Dumb Things Happen to Smart Companies," *Fortune,* June 23, 1997, pp. 159–60.

9. A. Sullivan, "Mobile Bets Drivers Pick Cappuccino over Low Prices," *Wall Street Journal,* February 30, 1995, pp. B1–B8.

10. Ibid.

11. Ibid.

12. A. Salpukas, "Gas-Station Designers Have Fantasies, Too," *New York Times,* May 25, 1997, section 4, p. 6.

13. R. Gibson, "Popular Pizza Chain's Gimmick Is Taste," *Wall Street Journal,* April 28, 1997, pp. B1, B3.

14. S. McCormack, "Making Waves," *Forbes,* April 5, 1999, pp. 76–81.

15. Ibid.

16. R. D. Hof, "What Every CEO Needs to Know about Electronic Business: A Survival Guide," *Business Week E.Biz,* March 22, 1999, pp. EB9–EB12.

17. A. Faircloth, "The Best Retailer You've Never Heard Of," *Fortune,* March 16, 1998, pp. 110–12.

18. Ibid.

19. E. Schonfeld, "A Site Where Hospitals Can Click to Shop," *Fortune,* April 12, 1999, p. 150.

CHAPTER 6

Designing Business Processes

"The goods are the same, yes. But the process of getting
them to the end user is undergoing radical reconstruction.
The process is rapidly becoming the product."
—Bob Bernabucci, President, UPS Capital Corporation

If a company is handicapped by incompetent employees, poorly designed and costly business processes, deficient quality programs, and insufficient information systems, then it will feel hard-pressed to deliver quality products and services at reasonable prices, and its customer value proposition will fail. One important determinant of customer value is operational effectiveness: a superior operating model, which is a collection of effective and efficient business processes. Good companies don't overengineer their operating model; they put the correct type and number of people to work in well-designed processes and support them with the best technology and quality programs available. Wal-Mart sells brand-name products at prices 2 percent to 4 percent less than its competitors because it has more efficient in-store operations, logistics systems, and warehousing operations. It is in control of its basic business processes and has a record of improving them over time.[1]

A business produces products and services through business processes. A business process is a set of sequential and coordinated activities that convert inputs into one or more outputs. It can be a work flow of material, people, information, and even knowledge. Examples of common business processes are new product or service development, which converts ideas into prototypes or pilots; accounts payable, which matches purchase orders, shipping notes, and invoices to produce checks and electronic payments; and order fulfillment, which begins with orders and ends when customers pay for products and services received. A business process can incorporate any combination of suppliers, people, technology, and customers. Suppliers provide the input; people perform some or all of the work; technology automates some or all of the process; and customers receive the output and judge the consequent value. Many business processes are cross-functional in nature, transcending the boundaries between various business functions, including sales, marketing, accounting, and customer service.

The overall design of a business process determines the

- bundle of benefits that constitute a product or service,
- extent of product or service differentiation,
- number and nature of activities performed to deliver the product or service,
- location of those activities,
- associated technologies and number of people involved,
- cost performance of the process, and
- degree of satisfaction experienced by customers.

Because the impact of a business process is so broad, companies should optimize their business processes rather than optimize the performance of their business functions. Customers are not interested in business functions per se; they're interested in the business processes with which they interface and the outcomes of those processes. Thus there is a need for true operational effectiveness. Companies can build operational effectiveness by gaining an enhanced understanding of the basic layout strategies for designing business processes and by applying a methodology that will improve any business process.

Layout Strategies for Business Processes

A layout strategy is the overall organization of the business process. It is highly affected by the volume processed and the degree of standardization of the product or service. A process-focused layout groups together similar activities. As a result, the employees and technologies are organized around particular activities. It is especially appropriate for customized low-volume products or services (see Figure 6.1). A product-focused layout sequences activities, employees, and technologies around the product or service to promote a smooth work flow. It's particularly effective for standardized

FIGURE 6.1
Business Process Layout Strategies

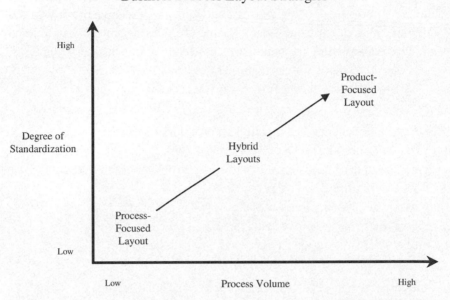

Source: This figure is a modified version of positioning strategies described by R. H. Hayes and S. C. Wheelwright, "Link Manufacturing Process and Product Life Cycles," *Harvard Business Review,* January–February 1979, pp. 133–140.

high-volume operations. Generally, companies employ both approaches separately or in combination.

For example, a retail bank performs a number of activities in serving its customers, including processing transactions and payments and rendering orders, which are performed by various areas or departments (see Figure 6.2). These activities can be organized into several core business processes; mortgage lending is one example (see Figure 6.3). Concerning mortgage lending, customers (i.e., loan applicants) enter a retail bank or branch office and speak either with front office personnel behind a counter, who may refer them to a mortgage specialist, or with the mortgage specialist directly. The mortgage specialist describes the available products and services, provides reading material, and fields any questions. If a customer makes a purchase decision, the specialist will also write the order. He or she sends the order to an underwriting agent in the mortgage lending

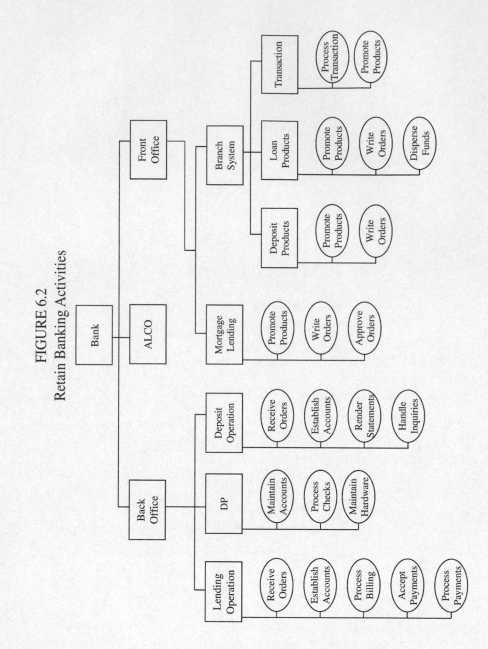

FIGURE 6.2
Retain Banking Activities

96

FIGURE 6.3
Mortgage Lending Activities

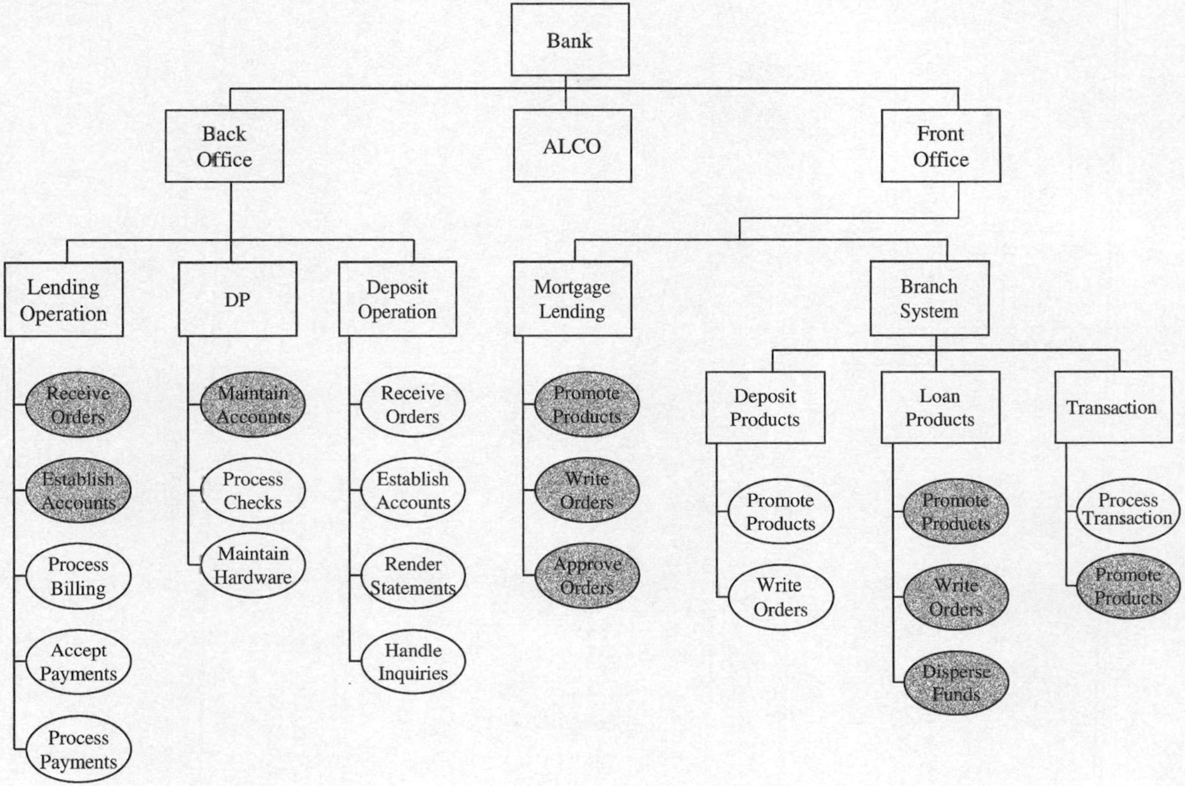

area, who evaluates the loan applicant and approves (or disapproves) the loan. If the mortgage loan is accepted, it moves to mortgage lending, a back office area that internally accepts the loan and establishes an account for it. When the funds are available, the mortgage specialist disperses the funds to the customer. In summary, the mortgage lending process is a core business process for a retail bank and it consists of a number of steps that are performed by people in several areas in different locations. The process cuts across traditional organizational structure, involving employees from different areas and departments to complete a piece of the overall work required. Consequently, each area makes its own unique contribution to the mortgage lending process.

The front office is process-focused because employees, activities, and materials are grouped according to specific products and services (e.g., personal loans, mortgage loans, and mutual funds). The services are customized and low-volume in nature. The back office is product-focused. Centralized functions, including check processing, savings record keeping, and loan processing, are standardized and high-volume. For example, the check processing function is organized to process each check in a batch, all in the same manner and as efficiently as possible.

A mortgage lending process that doesn't provide prospective customers with complete information on all available mortgages, requests additional applicant information after the order is written, makes customers wait more than a few days for a final decision, and is late in dispersing the funds will cause a retail bank to lose customers to other retail banks with a mortgage lending process that can provide those services more effectively. Additionally, the bank may lose the opportunity to sell other products and services. Consequently, companies must strive to create business processes that deliver considerable customer value, satisfying customers and driving margins up. But where does a company start? How does it proceed? This is a classic case where the devil is in the details.

Steps for Redesigning Business Processes

Companies need a systematic approach for beginning and managing the improvement of a business process. One methodology for improving an existing business process consists of six steps.

1. Define business direction.
2. Identify core business processes.
3. Develop deep process knowledge.
4. Learn from "world-class" standards.
5. Design a new business process.
6. Implement the new business process.[2]

The methodology entails setting business direction, developing a model of how a process works, recognizing important interfaces between functional areas, understanding customer needs, performing a benchmarking study, and implementing changes that would make a new business process successful. It is top-down in nature, customer-oriented, and, if followed, can help a company attain excellence. Companies must recognize that all business process redesign endeavors are risky. In fact, the chance of complete success may be only as high as 30 percent.[3] Companies fail for a variety of reasons, including lack of management support, inadequate software, and the inability to create organizational support for the requisite changes. Yet there are a number of steps that companies can take during implementation to mitigate the problems and increase their chances of success.[4]

Define Business Direction

Before companies can begin the task of improving their business processes, they first need to understand where they're going. One pertinent adage says, "If you don't know where you're going, any road will get you there." Companies need to state their business direction, namely a vision and/or mission, business goals, related strategies, and supporting business function objectives and strategies. With these elements in place, employees can begin on the road to designing processes that are congruent with their company's intentions. Companies don't want to invest in new processes that force them in the wrong direction. If low price is a dominating feature of a company's strategy, then it will be reflected in various goals, objectives, and strategies. It should be known to everyone so that employees create new processes that don't waste money. Thus the elements of business direction create a set of internal requirements that business processes need to satisfy. They also serve to govern the activities that take place on a daily basis. For example, knowing that a company is focused on providing responsive service, possibly measured by answering incoming telephone calls within four rings, gives employees targets as they conduct a process's activities.

Identify Core Business Processes

All companies have a set of core business processes that drive them forward. These core processes are fundamental to a company's operation and determine its ultimate success. Even the largest companies have no more than a dozen core business processes. Some core processes are relatively simple, whereas others are extremely complex. One team can perform certain processes, whereas other processes require multiple teams. A company's ability to produce customer value depends on how well these processes deliver the lowest-cost, highest-quality products and services to customers. Generally, a core process consumes a considerable amount of organizational energy, making it readily identifiable in most cases. (Surprisingly, some companies actually have a difficult time articulating their core business processes.) For example, in addition to mortgage lending, a retail bank has the following core processes.

- Consumer lending
- Commercial lending
- Investment
- Purchase funds management
- Product/service management
- Sales
- Customer service
- Product development

In a typical retail bank, it's highly likely that some of these processes are not operating at "world-class" levels. In dealing with the bank, the difficulties that customers experience are the result of management's inability to recognize underperforming processes and to rethink their layout strategy and execution.

Companies need to identify all core business processes, understand their relative priority, isolate the ones that lack operational effectiveness, and take the steps necessary to improve them. Managers should ask the following questions.

- What are the processes that have the greatest impact on customer value creation?
- What are the processes that have the highest visibility with customers?
- What are the processes that accelerate positive results?
- What are the processes that account for the major portion of the company's costs or revenues?

The answers to these questions depend on a company's business direction, its value proposition, its customers' satisfaction with the products and services provided, and its existing level of operational effectiveness vis-à-vis the competition.

Prioritizing processes is especially important. A company cannot redesign all of the business processes that may merit change, especially at the same time, because it's too disruptive to the organization, given the scope and scale of certain processes. With a prioritized list, a company can pick the one or two processes (hopefully low risk) that have the greatest impact on customer satisfaction and/or business performance (i.e., payback) to tackle first (see Figure 6.4). By taking this deliberate approach, companies will create a manageable environment, increasing their chances of success.

Develop Deep Process Knowledge

Many managers and employees fail to grasp the fact that they are part of a large system that serves numerous customers, is made up of multiple activities, crosses multiple business functions, and operates with a certain level of acceptable performance. A company without a systems mentality (for example, the ability to perceive a business process as a set of interrelated components) may not be able to articulate how some of its processes execute, primarily because each employee is working in a business function area on only a small part of the entire process.[5] For each process that is targeted for

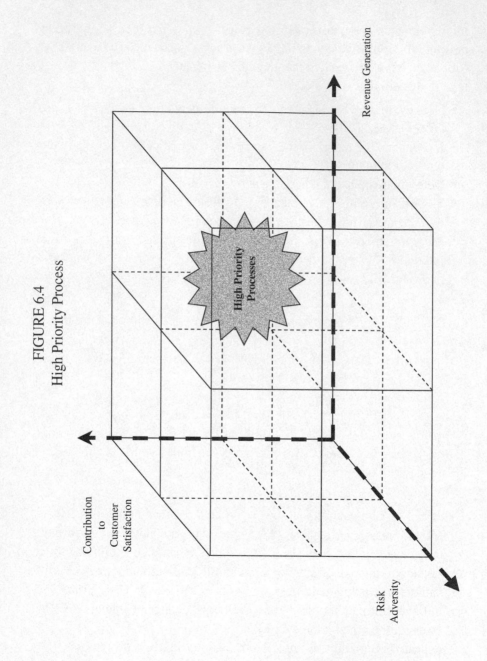

FIGURE 6.4
High Priority Process

102

improvement, a company needs to perform an in-depth process analysis to develop a thorough understanding of the process's activities and overall performance. It can do this by taking the following steps.

- Define company's and customers' requirements (i.e., needs and expectations).
- Understand the nature of the gap between actual performance and current requirements.
- Determine when and where the activities occur.
- Identify the entities (e.g., business functions) involved with the process.
- Identify the critical interface between each entity.
- Measure and document the process's performance with regard to the internal and external requirements imposed on the process by the company and its customers, respectively.

The successful execution of these steps provides an understanding of who's (namely employees, business functions, customers, suppliers, and partners) involved, what's happening, when it's happening, where it's happening, and why performance is the way it is.

Some managers and consultants advocate that all you need is a blank piece of paper to begin the redesign. This is a gross understatement! All companies need a good understanding of the baseline situation. By comparing the baseline against a new design to be implemented at a later time, companies get a complete picture of

- the degree of organizational change required, including new roles, new responsibilities, reporting line changes, and number of employees affected;
- amount of education and training required to prepare employees;
- impact on the existing process, including number and type of modifications to existing activities;
- initial investment required and incremental change in annual operating costs to implement the new process;
- expected improvement imparted by various alternate designs;
- after implementation, actual improvement attained versus baseline and expected improvement of alternate designs.

By juxtaposing the baseline situation against a new process design, a company can begin considering the tradeoffs in benefits to customers versus associated costs. Moreover, management can better understand the issues associated with a phased implementation of the new process. None of this is possible unless a company knows its starting point.

There are a number of good techniques for describing a process in understandable terms, including flow diagrams, which trace the flow of people, material, and equipment; process charts, which record activities, their sequence, and associated times; and service maps, which show all the process's sequenced activities.[6] A service map for one simplified order entry and fulfillment process would consist of the following activities: enter order; determine if merchandise is available; check customer credit; and create a packing slip and mailing label (see Figure 6.5).[7] The map may indicate critical tasks, activities most likely to fail, and other pertinent aspects of the process. It may also include current performance measurements (e.g., percent of orders unclear). The service map is one of the most popular methods for portraying a service process, and a number of software packages support the technique. With a service map, analysts can

- identify the participants in the process, including people, functional areas, and other entities,
- portray the activities and steps associated with the process,
- show the critical interfaces or boundary activities among various entities,
- identify ineffective and inefficient steps,
- document performance at critical steps and for the process as a whole, and
- cite specific work instructions.

Thus a service map is an important tool for portraying the intricate activities of a process, displaying its important contributors, and examining its current performance.

For a given process, a company's value proposition and its objectives and strategies help define several appropriate performance measures. They also help the company understand how it is currently performing vis-à-vis customers' expectations. For example, if the value proposition for the order entry and fulfillment process includes responsiveness and reliability as important components of customer value, then the percentage of orders handled

FIGURE 6.5
Order Entry and Fulfillment Process

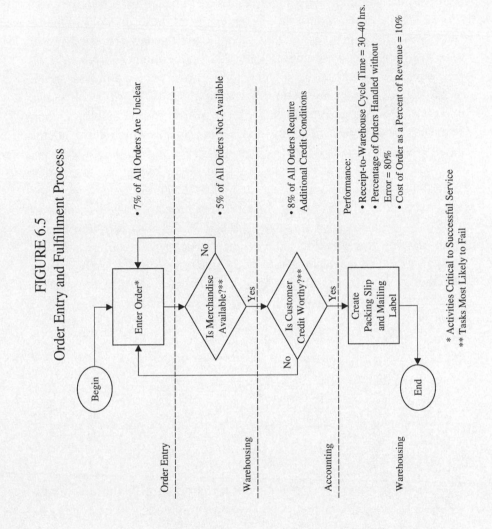

* Activities Critical to Successful Service
** Tasks Most Likely to Fail

105

without error and fulfillment cycle time (excluding shipping) may be two important measures for the process. The actual objectives for the process may be 95 percent error-free orders and just two hours for the order entry and fulfillment cycle time, respectively. Moreover, the company may have an internal objective for the cost of completing and filling an order, such as cost of entering and filling an order should be 5 percent of the average price of merchandise sold. An in-depth analysis of the process will reveal actual performance and identify some activities that may be responsible for poor performance. In reality, the process's actual performance may be far from the requirements imposed by customers and the company.

Learn from "World-Class" Standards

In a world of constant and rapid change, no single company dominates all "best practices." Good companies are constantly on the prowl for the "best" operating practices and most innovative ideas. Consequently, a number of companies make benchmarking an important part of their ongoing improvement efforts.

Benchmarking is the process of searching for, selecting, analyzing, and possibly adopting "best-in-class" practices, innovative ideas, and effective operating procedures to improve business performance.[8] With benchmarking, companies usually compare their processes, practices, products, and/or services against "best-in-class" companies (or at the very least superior companies) to understand the gaps between their practices and those of the benchmarked companies. Thus benchmarking is essentially an outreach activity that helps companies learn how to do things better. There are three types of benchmarking.

- Process benchmarking. Process benchmarking concentrates on business processes, including order entry, customer service, and new product development. The approach attempts to identify the best operating practices from one or more companies in any industry.
- Performance benchmarking. Companies that use performance benchmarking compare their products and/or services against their competitors on a number of performance characteristics or indicators, including price, technical quality (for products), and response time (for services).

Generally, they use direct comparisons, operating statistics, and reverse engineering to perform the benchmarking. With performance benchmarking, a company can identify performance standards that its competitors meet and customers expect.
- Strategic benchmarking. Strategic benchmarking focuses on uncovering exceptional business lessons and winning strategies rather than on identifying best operating practices or on comparing products and services against performance characteristics. A company seeks to identify new ways of competing, new business models, and new paradigms that have long-term consequences for the business.[9]

Concerning performance standards derived through performance benchmarking of competitors, many companies have a policy of meeting those standards rather than exceeding them. Companies shouldn't consider these performance standards to be upper limits; rather, they should be viewed as minimally acceptable levels of performance, simply because the benchmark companies and the competition get better over time.

Companies can benchmark processes, performance, and strategies against the following entities.

- similar functions in different business units (for example, accounts payable at GE Medical Systems versus accounts payable at GE Aircraft Engines);
- direct competitors (even the toughest) in the same markets with competing products and services;
- companies in the same industry with the same products and services, but serving different markets (for example, Kroger versus Hannaford food stores); and
- generic processes (for example, order entry) in any industry or company.

These activities are known as internal, competitive, functional, and generic benchmarking, respectively.

To abolish one management misconception, benchmarking does not mean that a company adopts a "best practice" in its pure form. Benchmarking involves thoughtful identification, examination, and analyses to understand why another company has been remarkably successful when others have not. Companies must creatively adapt their understanding of effective operating practices to their own specific situation. Additionally, an ongoing benchmarking program is an excellent method for staying current and not getting ambushed by the competition.

At times, obtaining collaboration from the benchmarked companies is difficult, especially with direct competitors, unless there is a quid pro quo and confidentiality issues are fully understood and upheld. Yet this shouldn't dissuade companies from benchmarking, because both companies benefit from an exchange of ideas.

Design a New Business Process

With knowledge of its business direction, the results of its in-depth process analysis, and the benefits of its benchmarking efforts, a company can begin the process of designing a new business process. This is a difficult step and it requires exceptional creativity. Everyone involved with the effort needs to challenge long-standing assumptions about work arrangements, traditional roles and responsibilities, relevant technologies, and so on. In some cases, the baseline process appears so complex that real breakthroughs seem impossible. Nevertheless, the previous steps build a foundation for moving forward. Business direction provides goals (often "stretch goals" or quantum leaps in performance) to pursue, the process analysis helps identify causes of poor performance that need to be corrected, and benchmarking indicates potential opportunities for doing things differently.

Information technology is often the enabling element for many new business systems and should influence alternate designs from the very start. There are a number of instances where the successful application of information technology has resulted in enormous process improvements. Consider the aforementioned order entry and fulfillment process. "Best-in-class" computer-based order entry and fulfillment systems equip a customer service associate with the necessary tools to increase accuracy of orders and speed their fulfillment (see Figure 6.6). For example, an intelligent order entry system would not admit incorrect data, including item numbers, item descriptions, and prices. The system would supply hooks to remote databases so the associate can check the availability (i.e., balance on hand) of

FIGURE 6.6

Redesigned Order Entry and Fulfillment Process

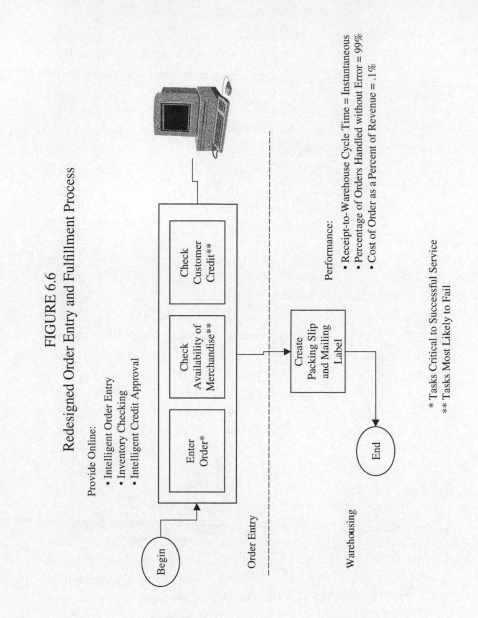

Provide Online:
- Intelligent Order Entry
- Inventory Checking
- Intelligent Credit Approval

Begin

Order Entry

| Enter Order* | Check Availability of Merchandise** | Check Customer Credit** |

Warehousing

Create Packing Slip and Mailing Label

End

Performance:
- Receipt-to-Warehouse Cycle Time = Instantaneous
- Percentage of Orders Handled without Error = 99%
- Cost of Order as a Percent of Revenue = .1%

* Tasks Critical to Successful Service
** Tasks Most Likely to Fail

109

merchandise. This capability ensures that nothing gets promised that can't be delivered and, by conveying an out-of-stock situation, customers get the opportunity to select substitutes or place items on backorder. Similarly, an intelligent credit appraisal system could check a customer's credit rating or determine the customer's credit worthiness in real time to avoid potential delays in filling the order. Finally, after recording the order, the system would produce a packing slip and mailing label. These capabilities prevent customers from being disappointed, increasing customer satisfaction, and they keep costs low by avoiding previous snafus in the delivery of the product.

Cost justifying various alternative designs is an essential part of this step. Few companies will accept a design based upon strategic considerations alone. For a specific design, cost justification involves two steps:

1. estimating savings and/or increased revenues as well as the associated startup and annual expenses of operating the new or redesigned process; and
2. for a given time frame, determining the net present value of the resulting cash flow at some interest rate or internal hurdle rate.

Few companies use a time frame of more than a few years to evaluate a new process design, because the pace of change is so rapid. Completely new business models can eclipse redesigned business processes in just a few years. One company uses a payback period of just two years for all projects: if the redesign effort doesn't generate enough cash to pay for itself in two years, then the investment isn't made, or other alternatives are investigated. Cash flow statements are one method of comparing the financial benefits (i.e., increased revenue, lower costs, and so on) and costs associated with alternate designs (see Figure 6.7). They're simple and straightforward and express major considerations in terms of hard numbers.

Implement the New Business Process

When a particular design passes the financial and business hurdles, companies need to implement it. Implementation is a critical step, considering that approximately 40 percent to 70 percent of all implementations are less successful than envisioned.[10] Yet this is understandable, because a new

FIGURE 6.7
Cash Flow Statement for Evaluating
Technology-Enabled New Processes

Projected Cash Flow	Scenario 1		
Statement	2000	2001	2002
Sales			
Cost of Goods Sold			
Gross Margin			
Technology Expenses			
Licensing Costs			
Salaries for Technical Staff			
Other Expenses			
Salaries for Nontechnical Staff			
Marketing Expenses			
Depreciation			
Operating Expenses			
EBIT			
Interest Charges			
Earnings before Taxes			
Income Taxes			
Net Income			
Depreciation			
After-Tax Cash Flow			
Net Present Value (NPV)			

design may mean a dramatic change to an existing business process. The new design may require the elimination of hierarchical levels, resulting in less supervision; empowerment of employees, who have to change their roles and take on more decision-making responsibilities; new work flows; the incorporation of new computer technologies and information systems, which have to be mastered; the collection and management of more data and information; and higher levels of data accuracy (which can be extremely difficult to attain and maintain, especially in an undisciplined organization). The redesign may significantly impact the way customers are encountered, changing the type of employee required to perform the work. To be successful, a company must take a number of steps and perform several activities as follows:

- Form a steering committee to oversee the project and provide the requisite resources.
- Prepare a detailed project plan to coordinate and control the multitude of steps associated with a project.
- Perform a detailed requirements analysis to understand and document all of the process's requirements and provide a foundation for selecting computer software.
- Achieve milestones early to stay on track and demonstrate progress.
- Develop and institute new policies and procedures.
- Develop new roles and responsibilities for new activities.
- Change staffing levels.
- Invest in new software that satisfies all of the process's requirements.
- Provide extensive education and training to prepare employees for their new roles and responsibilities (see Table 6.1).

In some cases, the degree of change may be so significant that it merits a complete cultural change in the organization, which extends beyond the installation period of the project. For example, middle managers and supervisors may have to change from being hierarchical bosses to builders of business, coaches, trainers, and so on. This process may take several years, and some employees may not be capable of changing. Companies that are just starting out should consider projects that have a low risk of failure, unless forced to do otherwise by competitive necessity. The best way to win management and organization support is to start a project that will demonstrate positive results early on.

Redesigning Business Processes at Kitware Incorporated

Kitware develops advanced visualization, graphics, and image processing software for a number of applications, including engineering, medical imaging, and aerospace. The Visualization Toolkit (VTK) is the base software for

TABLE 6.1
List of Steps and Activities for
Implementing a New Business Process

- Form a steering committee
- Form a project team
- Perform a cost/benefit analysis
- Make it a high priority
- Provide timely education and training at all levels
- Use formal project planning
- Develop clear objectives
- Reengineer or design business processes
- Develop formal policies and procedures
- Perform requirements analysis
- Select the "best" software and vendors
- Accomplish target dates
- Gain control of data and increase accuracy
- Implement system and institute formal policies, procedures, and controls
- Show early benefits
- Distribute roles and responsibilities
- Integrate the system with operations and provide rapid turnaround
- Hold people accountable
- Use multiple performance measures

the company's two primary products, VolView and the *VTK User's Guide*.
VTK source code is available free of charge to researchers and software
developers interested in visualization software. Generally, computer scientists and other technical specialists work with VTK directly. VolView is a
general-purpose volume visualization application for Windows 95/98 NT,
Linux, and Unix platforms. It contains volume visualization features, including easy-to-use transfer functions, material editors, shading capabilities, and cropping and cutting tools. Engineering, aerospace, and medical

personnel, who are not interested in the underlying VTK code but in the application of the combined VolView and VTK software to solve real-world problems, are the typical end users. A demo version of VolView is available for a thirty-day evaluation. If the software is purchased, Kitware provides the customer with an activation code, which allows unlimited use. The *VTK User's Guide* describes how to use and extend VTK and includes detailed examples, installation procedures, and file format descriptions. In addition to VolView and the *VTK User's Guide,* Kitware also provides consulting, training, and support services.

Kitware's initial order fulfillment process was cumbersome, resource-intensive, and time-consuming (see Figure 6.8). Many of the activities and tasks involved manual processing of payments, manual entry of data, and manual distribution of software and activation codes. To order products or services, such as VolView or the *VTK User's Guide,* Kitware required customers to print an order form from its server. A customer completed the form and either faxed, mailed, or phoned in the order, which included payment in the form of a credit card number (or a check for some mail orders). For a *VTK User's Guide* order, after processing the order's payment, Kitware entered the order, customer, and shipping information into its system and printed a bill of lading and mailing label for the order. Although VTK and VolView were available from Kitware's server, the company burned copies of VTK on a CD and packaged it with the *VTK User's Guide.* It mailed the entire package to the customer. For a VolView order, Kitware used the same approach to process the order-related information, but phoned the customer to convey the activation code that would allow continued use of VolView.

With a complete understanding of the customers' requirements and of the initial process, Kitware performed benchmarking by examining the approaches of a number of well-trusted online stores, including Vitalogy, Yahoo! Store, and GeoCities. A cost justification analysis of the new process with each online store considered separately indicated that Net-Sales had a slightly higher return than the other candidates considered. (NetSales is a full service, e-commerce solutions provider that manages the complexity of online sales for its customers.) Kitware revamped the initial order fulfillment process, making it less resource-intensive and giving customers almost immediate access to unlimited VolView functionality. The

FIGURE 6.8
Kitware's Initial Order Fulfillment System

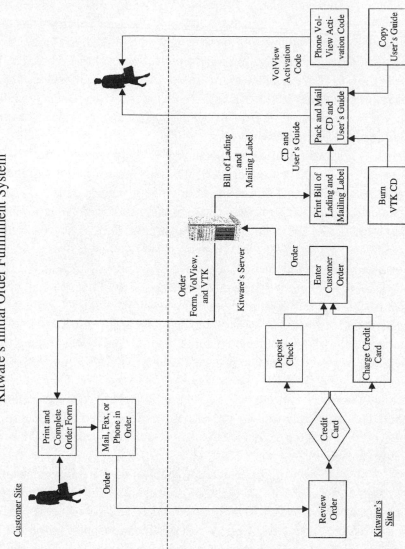

new process improved the overall effectiveness and efficiency of filling orders, satisfying both the customers' and company's requirements.

In the new process, a customer completes an order online (see Figure 6.9). Kitware eliminated the manual processing of orders and payments by having NetSales process them. NetSales handles the order by processing the credit card number or wire transfer and, after payment authorization is received from the customer's bank, by sending the pertinent order information to Kitware. The order information sent to Kitware excludes the credit card number of the customer. This allows Kitware to free itself of the security issues associated with maintaining online credit card numbers. In the new process, special software will process the NetSales order information, updating Kitware's internal order, customer, and shipping files; sending e-mail to notify the customer that the software and manual are in transit; and sending an encrypted activation code for unlimited use of VolView. According to Kitware, the new process allows the company to

- eliminate the need to take credit card information;
- eliminate the need to manually enter customer and shipping information (e.g., e-mail address, billing address, and shipping address);
- offer more methods of shipping, including FedEx, UPS, and US Postal Service because the print mailing label activity is automatic and flexible; and
- immediately issue the VolView activation code electronically.

For customers who do not want to download VTK, Kitware will continue to burn the software onto a CD. This approach helps customers with slower connections to better manage the large data sets that accompany the software. To minimize unlimited copying and distribution of the *User's Guide,* Kitware will continue to produce and distribute the guide in hardcopy form. However, the company is considering online distribution of the guide at this time. In a world where all products are in electronic form, the cost of distributing them drops to almost zero. The implementation plan is phased over time. The current plan is to bring NetSales on board, followed by an implementation of the special software that processes an order completely.

FIGURE 6.9
Kitware's New Order Fulfillment System

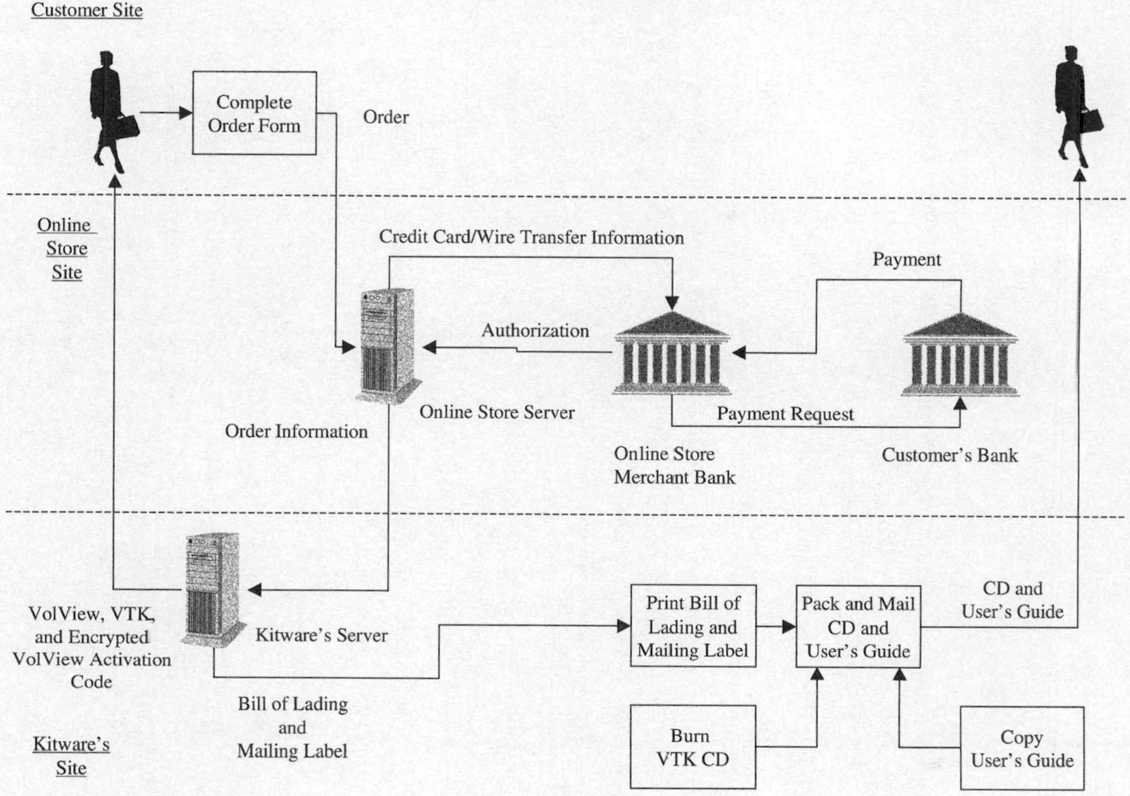

Management Directives

The methodology and the examples previously described provide managers with several directives to consider.

- Build operational effectiveness. A company's ability to deliver its value proposition is directly dependent on its operating model. Companies need well-engineered business processes that directly support their value proposition. For example, in Web-based businesses, the companies that can implement an operationally effective combination of front-end (e.g., information sharing, ordering, and payment systems), back-end logistics, and after-sales customer support systems will be successful. The business processes that a company utilizes determine the content of the service package, extent of differentiation, and the cost of the final product or service.
- To build operational effectiveness, follow a systematic approach. To improve business processes, companies need to use a comprehensive approach that considers business direction, focuses on customers, analyzes all activities, and incorporates benchmarking data drawn from numerous sources. By touching all of the right bases, a company can increase the chance of successively implementing the best possible business process for itself.
- Prioritize processes. At the beginning, companies should select the processes with the lowest risk and highest impact on the business to focus improvement efforts. If management and organizational support are suspect, companies should select a process that will demonstrate early positive results to build support and get an entry in the win column. At all times, the number of projects should be controlled so as not to overwhelm a company. Many companies sink because they take on too much too soon.
- Understand the baseline. All companies should develop a thorough understanding of the existing situation. Knowing the starting point helps companies estimate and plan for the changes required to realize an improved business process. Additionally, with an explicit baseline, companies can better analyze the benefit and cost tradeoffs associated with alternate designs.
- Incorporate benchmarking. Companies need to make benchmarking an important part of all improvement activities. The free exchange of information can provide new ideas and lead to a creative business process.

- Shoot for the moon, but insist on discipline. Companies should strive for quantum leaps in performance in a new process. Yet this is extremely difficult to do, because it requires tremendous creativity and the ability to change management and organizational inertia. In many cases, information technology will be an enabling element because of its potential to eliminate steps and provide valuable information to decision makers. Management should insist that all new processes demonstrate significant payback. Good ideas alone are insufficient; they have to make money as well.
- Implement with a good plan. Implementation of a new business process may require significant change in process activities, roles, responsibilities, computer systems, and so on. To be successful during implementation, companies should provide the requisite resources and set measurable short-term objectives in their project plans so that implementation problems can be identified and corrected quickly. A cultural change may be needed, but through education and the appropriate reward systems a company can get the job done.

Notes

1. "Wal-Mart Stores, Inc.," Harvard Business School Case (9-794-024), revised in 1996.
2. This methodology resembles a six-step methodology proposed by T. R. Furey. See T. R. Furey, "A Six-Step Guide to Process Reengineering," *Planning Review,* March–April 1993, pp. 20–23.
3. M. Hammer and S. A. Stanton, *The Reengineering Revolution* (New York: Harper Collins, 1995).
4. The author describes these steps at the end of this chapter.
5. Manufacturing companies usually have well-documented processes. Service companies are generally less formal with regard to process documentation.
6. Almost any good operations management text contains a description of these techniques. For example, see R. S. Russell and B. W. Taylor, III, *Operations Management,* 3d ed. (Upper Saddle River, N.J.: Prentice Hall, 1998).
7. A real service map for this process would contain many more activities.
8. For more information on benchmarking, see R. C. Camp, *Benchmarking: The Search for Industry Best Practices* (Milwaukee, Wis.: ASQC Press, 1989).

9. "Benchmarking for Best Practices: Winning Through Innovative Adaptation," <www.benchmarkingreports.com/book/benchmarking_book_chapter1.htm>, accessed November 29, 1999.

10. Michael Hammer suggests that the rate of failure may be as high as 70 percent. However, the author's experience indicates that it's much lower, especially if companies take the steps indicated in Table 6.1.

CHAPTER 7

Managing People for Positive Results

"To the extent that auto insurance is a commodity, our biggest differentiator is our people. We want the best people at every level of the company, and we pay at the top of the market."

—Peter Lewis, CEO and Chairman, Progressive Corporation

People develop a company's plans, execute them, and serve customers. As a result, people are an especially critical asset. All companies interact with customers and the nature of the encounter is extremely important, because it is at this point that customers form opinions about those companies, including their reliability, competence, accessibility, and so on. Successful encounters beget customer satisfaction, create trust, and build loyalty. Johnson Controls manages energy systems, including heating, lighting, and security systems, at customer sites. The company also makes many of the components that go into energy systems. Its field personnel and engineers solve customer problems, look for ways to save customers money, and help customers reduce downtime. The nature of the work demands employees who are empathetic, flexible, informative, innovative, articulate, communicative, and willing to work as team players, have a sense of humor, and are capable of working with little supervision. How does a company develop this type of employee? How does a company get people to do what they are supposed to do without being told to do so? How does a company motivate employees, at every level, to embrace the skills and attitudes necessary to satisfy and exceed customers' needs and expectations? None of this is easy, precisely because people are complex.

To build a cadre of effective employees, companies must do the following.

121

- Select the correct employees.
- Provide them with leadership via a mission statement, business goals, business function objectives, and related strategies so that employees are aware of the company's intentions.
- Educate and train employees so that they are fully capable of doing their jobs.
- Support employees with the best business processes and information technologies.
- Empower employees to fully apply their skills and act on behalf of the customers.
- Measure employee performance to provide feedback and indicate progress toward goals and objectives.
- Provide employees with appropriate compensation and recognition.

As indicated, compensation isn't the only factor that requires consideration, as some managers wrongly believe. In fact, pay ranks behind senior management leadership and the chance to use one's skills as a driver of employee commitment.[1] A company that follows the directives listed can develop a culture that is capable of being customer-oriented, carrying out a new strategy, adding value to customers, and exhibiting the appropriate behavior at all times.

Selecting the Correct People

Good companies put extraordinary emphasis on the recruiting process. Beginning with the "very best" people is extremely important. The features that define "very best" generally vary across job categories. For example, the criteria for selecting software engineers (e.g., ability to attack problems) may be different from those for selecting call center personnel (e.g., ability to dispel customer anger). Companies have to elucidate the important job criteria and develop a rigorous selection methodology to make sure they obtain the most appropriate employees. Resume screening, psychological testing, problem solving, role-playing, and interviews with line managers, peers, and human resource specialists may constitute part or all of the selection methodology.

At Southwest Airlines there is general recognition that competitors can acquire basic tangible assets, including planes, gates at airports, and baggage handling equipment. The key to success at Southwest Airlines is the "spirit," or culture, which is a fragile, intangible asset that can't be duplicated as easily as the physical assets. If the company loses it, it will have lost its most valuable competency. According to Southwest management, employee recruitment is a primary reason for the company's enviable esprit de corps. The company begins with people who have the right attitude, a sense of humor, and like other people. The company feels that it can train employees to do their jobs, but it can't change innate attitudes. With a clear understanding of a job's specific requirements (for instance, behavior, knowledge, and motivation), Southwest solicits applications. After it receives the applications, data entry clerks key in basic information, which allows recruiters to sort by any criteria to narrow down the field of potential candidates. For flight attendants, a group review screens applicants, asking them to share their backgrounds. After passing the group review, applicants complete three one-on-one interviews: with a recruiter, supervisor, and a peer. Two criteria that are especially relevant to flight attendants are judgment and teamwork. Consequently, interviewers will ask questions to ascertain how a candidate makes decisions in specific situations. The intensive interview process lasts about six weeks and it consists of five parts:

1. use past behavior to predict future behavior,
2. identify critical job requirements,
3. apply effective interviewing,
4. involve several interviewers, and
5. augment interviews with behavioral simulations.

By applying rigorous recruitment and selection processes, the company acquires employees that generate enthusiasm, are playful—even after long hours on the job—and serve the customer with a smile.[2]

Providing Leadership

Companies need to tell their employees exactly what's expected of them. They can do this through the mission statement, business goals and strategies, and functional objectives and strategies. The mission statement helps employees understand what they should be doing on a daily basis. Goals and objectives convey what the company hopes to achieve for its customers, employees, and stockholders. Business and functional area strategies describe how the company should attain its goals and objectives. Together, these elements of business direction give employees purpose, foster cohesion, provide a sense of uniqueness, impart methods for pursuing the mission and achieving goals and objectives, and furnish a context for each employee to grasp his or her own role and responsibilities in the greater enterprise.

Some companies augment these elements of business direction with general philosophies or themes. For example, L.L. Bean's philosophy is

A customer is the most important person in person or by mail. A customer is not dependent on us, we are dependent on him. A customer is not an interruption of our work, he is the purpose of it.[3]

FedEx creates common purpose with a straightforward theme: "Absolutely, positively overnight!"

Managers can also demonstrate leadership by exhibiting the appropriate behavior in front of employees at all times. For example, if service quality is important, returning phone calls or e-mail promptly, being affable and respectful to employees and customers, and getting out of the office to witness and constructively comment on frontline activities are actions that send the right message. Through their words and actions, managers are constantly sending signals to their employees and prompting certain behaviors. Asking a company to behave in one way and acting in another leads to confusion and results in management's intentions not being taken seriously by employees.

Almost all companies, both fledgling and mature, have one or more of the basic elements of business direction in place. The key is to bring them down to earth so employees can understand and commit to them. Companies need to communicate the business direction elements (i.e., mission, goals, business function objectives, and associated strategies) thoroughly to all employees. Companies that continually share their business intentions and actual progress with employees can engender a sense of shared values, instill a common purpose, and create a sense of commitment among individuals at all levels of the organization. Hewlett-Packard (HP) holds "coffee talks" on a regular basis, where management discusses the activities and performance of certain areas and the company as a whole with all employees. The company believes that employees should have a view that goes beyond their own narrow perspectives and specialties.[4] Without disseminating business direction, a company just has a lot of words on paper. Good companies promulgate their intentions to people at all levels so as to resonate across the entire company.

Educating and Training Employees

Education and training is another important determinant for developing quality employees. Employees can't be expected to do a good job without adequate preparation, induced by education, training, and experience. This is a difficult concept for many companies to grasp because they have a difficult time discerning the immediate, direct benefit of education and training expenses. Unlike physical assets (e.g., equipment), the result of education and training is intangible in nature and may manifest itself only gradually. Yet investing in the education and training of employees is essential. Research demonstrates that a 10 percent increase in workforce education level leads to an almost 9 percent increase in productivity. A 10 percent rise in plant and equipment values results in just a 3 percent to 4 percent increase in productivity.[5]

As a result, good companies emphasize education and training throughout the company. The Ritz-Carlton employs a rigorous orientation and training certification program to offer better service with fewer employees. The company's commitment to employee training is one reason why it has won the Malcolm Baldrige National Quality Award twice since 1992 and why its employee turnover rate is five times less than the industry average. During their first two days, all employees meet members of upper management, enjoy a meal as "guests" in a hotel dinning room, and learn the company's standards, philosophy, expectations, values, and benefits. The company believes that it is important for all employees to adopt the company's approach in order to uphold its arduous service standards. After orientation, trainers partner with employees to help them through the workday. After three weeks, new employees talk about their experiences while managers listen closely to ensure that everyone is on track with the company's philosophy. During the first year, employees amass 310 hours of training and 100 hours of training each subsequent year. The monthly or quarterly classes include "Appreciating Individual Differences," "Planning and Running Team Meetings," and "Assessing Your Coworker's Performance."[6]

Companies shouldn't be hesitant to go beyond the basic education and training required by employees to do their jobs. Education and training for developing critical thinking skills, working in a team environment, and communicating effectively are also important to employees and allow them to contribute on a grander scale. For example, the activities of designing innovative services, implementing information technology, and solving business problems generally occur in a team setting. The teams consist of individuals drawn from a range of disciplines and organizational levels and focus on specific tasks, business issues, or projects. These teams are especially effective when their members have both analytical and social skills.

Companies may also need to educate and train employees in other companies who interface with their customers. To provide better service to retail customers, Owens Corning provided training on products and services to salespeople on the floor at retailers, such as Lowes and Home Depot, who sometimes hire people who know little more than the shoppers.[7] Companies use onsite instruction, training videos, and reading materials to make salespeople more knowledgeable about their products and more effective in dealing with their customers.

All companies should view people as a source of intellectual capital (for example, thoughts, ideas, information, and service) that makes their businesses successful. Most people want to be productive, grow, contribute to a cause, and feel part of a team. Many companies are discovering that education and training enable employees to self-actualize along these lines. As a result, some companies have corporate universities, which provide courses to build the knowledge and skills to keep them competitive. For example, Motorola University spends $95 million a year to provide approximately 2,000 courses to its employees.[8] Not all companies need to go this far. Companies with fewer resources can develop smaller-scale programs or reimburse employees for courses taken externally. If a company isn't helping to enrich employees, then it shouldn't be surprised when they go elsewhere or fail to perform as expected. According to a Gallup survey, baby boomers, Generation X employees, and senior employees alike value employer-sponsored education and training programs. In fact, they are more likely to stay with a company that invests in such programs. Computer, communication, and management skills top the list of desired skills, especially for the Generation X employees.[9] This isn't surprising, because in most businesses today, the key to advancement is what one knows.

Providing a Supportive Business Process

Companies can take a lot of pressure off their employees with well-designed business processes that are enabled with the pertinent information technology. By giving employees a formal process, information, and analytical capability to identify customers, solve problems, and answer questions, companies can significantly increase the likelihood of successful service encounters. Just consider a typical call center, one of the most high-pressured functions in any business. Employees at call centers must soothe angry customers and solve their problems while being patient and polite even when the caller is not. They have to master administrative and technical details and explain them in layman's terms. Finally, they may have as many as 100 customer service episodes each day, five days per week. It's no easy job.

Companies can reduce the stress of the job and maintain high levels of customer satisfaction with a well-designed process that allows customers to help themselves and offers human assistance when self-help fails. Companies can support call center employees by giving them electronic access to customer information, including names, accounts, and problem or service histories; electronic manuals; frequently asked questions (FAQs); and search routines that identify a solution to a problem given key words, a rough description of the problem, and/or symptoms of the problem. They can also provide them with guidelines and support for referring a problem when it can't be addressed at their level.

Self-help functionality can ease the demands on call center staff by addressing common or recurring questions and problems. Generally, self-help capabilities are implemented on a Web site and include FAQs, access to customer accounts, and the ability to issue problem tickets and send e-mails to call center staff. Companies can provide the same functionality to their call center staff and augment it with even more powerful capabilities, such as the ability to hook into remote databases, perform key word searches of knowledge databases, and access symptom matrices that provide solutions to problems given specific symptoms. By giving call center staff fingertip access to the information and knowledge to effectively serve customers and by training them to transfer callers with complex questions to specialists, companies give employees a solid foundation for helping customers and increasing customer satisfaction.

For example, Motive Communications and Peregrine Systems offer electronic capabilities to create multitiered, real-time call center support. The first tier is self-service, whereas the second tier is the help desk, where the problem is logged into Peregrine's Service Center solution. Support analysts can use incident and system information supplied by Motive to diagnose the problem and provide solutions. Via the system, analysts can electronically refer more complex problems to on- or off-site experts. The consolidated approach permits employee self-empowerment solutions.[10]

Empowering Employees

When a company selects the correct people, provides leadership, educates and trains them appropriately, and supports them with an effective business process and information systems, it can empower them to act on behalf of the company and its customers. Without the proper preparation, empowerment just doesn't work. Companies that make all the correct moves benefit from empowerment because it puts control of the business in the hands of frontline employees who are closest to customers. These are the employees that sell, produce, deliver, support, and serve customers on a regular basis.

One of the keys to Wal-Mart's success is employee empowerment. Store managers have the authority to determine the type and amount of merchandise in a store, and store associates can participate in the Volume Producing Item (VPI) program, developing personalized displays within the store. Additionally, buyers include store associates in their decision making, especially if they're considering a change associates will have to implement.[11] Wal-Mart supports its employees by providing information on the top-selling items so they can position those items at the end of aisles for maximum exposure and increased sales.

Creating Measurement Systems

Once employees know what they're supposed to do, receive the requisite education and training, and have a well-designed business process behind them, a company needs to measure employee performance. "What gets measured gets done" is one of business's primary axioms. With an explicit value proposition and a set of goals and objectives in place, a company can implement measurement systems that give employees immediate feedback on the company's progress toward meeting customers' needs and expectations, on attaining business goals and business function objectives, and on their actual job performance. Companies can measure even soft criteria, such as customer satisfaction, using five-point rating or Likert scales. With feedback on actual job performance, employees can make the necessary adjustments to achieve stipulated targets.

MBNA, a credit card company, is devoted to serving its customers. Speed of service is an important component of the company's value proposition. Consequently, the company monitors its performance along this dimension with fifteen measures, many of them relating to speed, such as the following.

- Customer address changes must be processed in one day.
- Telephone must be answered within two rings.
- Switchboard calls must be transferred to the appropriate person within twenty-one seconds.

At any given moment, employees can view their performances down to tenths of a percent (e.g., two-ring pickup 98.5 percent of the time). Information systems enable speedy processing and close monitoring of actual service, allowing personnel to meet time commitments. For example, service representatives pass along requests for increased credit lines to the credit department, triggering an electronic time stamp. Managers can examine the number of queued requests and the amount of elapsed time for all requests. This makes it possible to shift requests among the various credit analysts in an effort to meet performance measures. Regarding the fifteen measures, the company posts its targets and actual performance on roughly sixty scoreboards at MBNA facilities around the country. So that speed doesn't become the overriding concern, the company also emphasizes other measures that relate to quality.[12]

Providing Adequate Compensation

After a company defines what its employees should do and learns how to measure system performance, they need to pay them accordingly. Let the employees who create value for customers and the business earn more money. There are a variety of compensation approaches and no overriding agreement as to which is the best one. A goal-focused program uses one or more performance measures—derived from business goals, objectives, strategies, and/or elements of a value proposition—and performance goals based on those measures. It pays employees additional money for attainment of performance goals. These variable pay, or pay-for-performance, programs align compensation with the goals and objectives of the business. They are distinctly different from and better than programs that base compensation on title or length of service.

Performance measures and their associated goals should be

- clear and supported by management;
- in close alignment with business needs;
- within an employee's control and, as a result, subject to his or her impact; and
- simple, easy to communicate, and clearly understood.

By establishing performance measures and associated goals, companies can align the employee activities with the business. Setting performance thresholds, the minimum level to qualify for additional pay, is tricky business: too low and a company may pay twice for expected results; too high and employees may just give up. At MBNA, for every day performance goals are met, the company contributes money to a pool for non-officers. If employees meet the goal 100 percent of the time, they share the contents of the pool at the end of the year. If employees meet the goal 75 percent of the time, they share a portion of the pool.[13]

Variable pay comes in different forms (e.g., increases in hourly rates, bonuses, and stock options), is distributed at different times of the year (e.g., at the end of the year or quarterly), and is recognized at various events. Competitive industry practice and corporate policies will determine which options are most appropriate.

Finally, all compensation schemes should reach as far down into the company as possible. Employees shouldn't have to move up to make more money. GE cut its salary grades from twenty-nine to six to give employees more opportunities to get raises without promotions. Additionally, GE increased the number of employees eligible for stock options.[14] Companies should recognize that employees at all levels, especially those below senior management, are responsible for making them successful. Twenty-eight companies on the 1999 list of the 100 best companies to work for in America offer stock options to every category of employee.[15]

Education and Training at Siemens Shared Services

Siemens is a large diversified electrical engineering and electronics company. Siemens Shared Services (S^3) organizes shared services centers, which provide leading-edge accounting services to Siemens business units (e.g., Siemens Power Generation) in the Pacific Rim, Europe, and the United States. The centers assume responsibility for processing all relevant accounting and logistics-related transactions that are entered by users at a business unit. The centers consider each business unit as a customer and have service level agreements (SLAs) in place to delineate responsibilities and ensure high levels of service quality.

A center uses templates, which are partially developed by accounting and information systems experts at corporate Siemens, to govern general ledger accounting, accounts receivable, accounts payable, and reporting processes. A template standardizes about 80 percent of a process. Business units customize the remaining 20 percent of the templates to satisfy unique accounting and reporting requirements of specific countries and/or geographic regions. Spiridon is S^3's SAP R/3-based implementation of the templates. The global templates, together with the local modifications made by a business collectively, represent the Spiridon application solution for the business unit. Relative to conventional practice, the benefits of the shared services approach include greater standardization of accounting entries, greater visibility of accounting data, and faster consolidation and reporting of business information.

S^3 Training, a part of Siemens Business Systems, is responsible for

- providing consultation on education and training to S^3 management;
- developing an integrated transformation training plan (ITTP); and
- providing and offering education and training programs to S^3 staff, a center's personnel, and managers and users at business units.

The ITTP is a comprehensive training concept that covers three types of education and training: task, people, and self (see Figure 7.1). Task-related education and training encompass technical (e.g., Spiridon and SAP R/3) and professional (Generally Accepted Accounting Principles [GAAP]) aspects of a job. People-related education and training includes leadership, conflict management, and service quality management issues, whereas self-related education and training covers self-management (e.g., time management) and career management (e.g., promotion) issues. Based on a "gap"

FIGURE 7.1
S^3 Training's Integrated Model of Training for Sustainable Performance

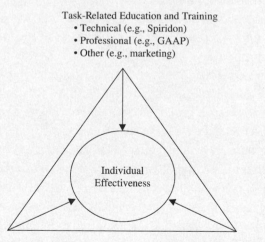

Task-Related Education and Training
  • Technical (e.g., Spiridon)
  • Professional (e.g., GAAP)
  • Other (e.g., marketing)

Individual Effectiveness

People-Related Education and Training
  • Management, Leadership, and Motivation
  • Conflict Management (e.g., communication)
  • Service and Quality Management

Self-Related Education and Training
  • Self-Management (e.g., stress management)
  • Appraisal (e.g., promotion)

Source: This figure is a modified version of a slide from an S^3 Training presentation.

analysis, S^3 Training develops a highly tailored education and training program for S^3 staff, center personnel, and users at business locations. S^3 Training experts perform the analysis, develop the integrated education and training programs, and perform the education and training at S^3, center, and user locations.

S^3 divides the implementation of a Spiridon application solution or customer solution into three phases: preparation, implementation, and operations and maintenance. During the preparation phase, S^3 Training's trainers provide a business unit's management with an introduction to the shared services concept, provide a Spiridon overview, describe the importance of management support during implementation, and explain the nature of the forthcoming organizational and process changes. S^3 Training's trainers perform the gap analysis to assess the education and training needs of the business unit and develop a complete education and training plan, which incorporates the task-, people-, and self-related aspects of the ITTP. The trainers perform all of the education and training during the implementation phase, which is divided into three primary stages: *Blueprint, Realization,* and *Go Live.*

During the first stage, *Blueprint,* S^3 Training selects a group of users to become power users. Over a two-to-three-week period, S^3 Training's trainers educate and train the power users on all aspects of the global template and make them proficient in using SAP R/3 to process some transactions. S^3 Training also selects a group of users to become internal SAP R/3 consultants. S^3 Training's trainers provide the SAP R/3 consultants with extensive education and training on SAP R/3 settings, which define the template in the SAP R/3 system. The education and training promotes buyin from both user groups. During the next phase, the members of these groups act as internal champions and on-site experts. During *Realization,* power users and SAP R/3 consultants work on customizing the remaining 20 percent of the templates to suit their local needs. After the business unit accepts the Spiridon application solution, it is transferred to a center for subsequent implementation. S^3 Training's trainers begin educating and training all users in the business unit. The training covers the task-, people-, and self-related issues that the trainers found to be important during their gap analysis. During the training sessions, as part of task-related education and training, users execute the Spiridon application solution to process actual business transactions. The entire process is modular in nature so those users can comprehend each process template in its entirety and understand its relationship to other process templates. During *Go Live,* all shared services become fully operational in the business unit.

Because users forget some of the initial education and training that they received during the operations and maintenance phase, S^3 Training's trainers provide refresher education and training. As S^3 staff creates new versions of the templates, there is a need for additional education and training, with a focus on the new enhancements. Thus education and training is a continuous process within the centers and business units. S^3 realizes that education and training are an important part of preparing employees to effectively do their jobs today and in the future.

Management Directives

The previous examples provided demonstrate that companies have a number of tools for ensuring positive service encounters. The salient points are as follows.

- Use a rigorous selection program. Companies can increase their chances of a positive service encounter by putting the "right" people in front of the customer. Finding Mr. or Ms. Right requires an effective selection methodology, which may use a combination of resume screening, psychological testing, problem solving, and other tools for becoming more knowledgeable about potential employees.
- Provide leadership and disseminate management's intentions. Companies have to give employees reasons for contributing on a daily basis. People want to be led, they want to achieve, and they want to be a part of grand undertakings. Managers can provide leadership via the various elements of business direction, namely the mission statement, business goals, and business function objectives and strategies. Personal actions taken by management and internal communication channels are also important. Through example, management can demonstrate leadership. Even the simplest acts (e.g., being cordial to customers) performed in front of employees send a strong signal. Formal communication channels provide a way to propagate business direction to all employees and keep them informed of a company's progress. Employees want to be informed.

- Provide education and training. To prepare companies to do their jobs correctly, companies have to provide education and training for new employees, and on a continuous basis, especially in areas (e.g., electronics) where the requisite knowledge may be increasing at an exponential rate. Good companies require employees to commit to a specified amount of education and training each year. Moreover, they are not hesitant to educate and train other companies' employees, especially if they directly or indirectly represent their products and services.
- Relieve pressure through a supportive business process. With a well-designed business process, companies can alleviate potential obstacles that prevent employees from effectively and efficiently serving customers. Well-designed business processes can reduce product defects and service nonconformities. Well-designed business processes consist of the correct activities, have the correct staffing, and use the appropriate technology.
- Take measurements and reward good performance. By measuring performance, companies can provide important feedback that lets employees know how they're doing and gives them time to make the adjustments necessary to achieve performance goals. Moreover, by creating a variable pay scheme, companies can reward the people who are adding value to customers and the company. A variable pay program shouldn't be just for management: everyone in the company should be eligible, especially those people who interface directly with customers.

Notes

1. G. Donnelly, "Recruiting, Retention, and Returns," *CFO The Magazine for Senior Financial Executives,* March 2000, pp. 68–70, 73.
2. B. P. Sunoo, "How Fun Flies at Southwest Airlines," *Personnel Journal* 74, no. 6 (June 1995), pp. 62–72.
3. This is an abridged version of the original philosophy.
4. A. Deutschman, "The Managing Wisdom of High-Tech Superstars," *Fortune,* October 17, 1994, pp. 197–206.
5. R. Donkin, "Value and Rewards of Brainpower," *Financial Times,* June 13, 1997, p. 1.
6. J. Elswick, "Puttin' on the Ritz: Hotel Chain Touts Training to Benefit Its Recruiting and Retention," *Securities Data Publishing Employee Benefit News,* February 1, 2000, pp. 1–4.

7. T. A. Stewart, "Owens Corning Back from the Dead," *Fortune,* May 26, 1997, pp. 118–26.

8. R. Brumer, "Why Companies Make Training a Major Priority," *Electronic News,* May 18, 1998, pp. 36–41.

9. *Arizona Business Gazette Retro Biz,* September 17, 1998, p. 2.

10. "Peregrine Systems Partners with Motive Communications to Offer IT Solutions That Enhance Employee Self-service," <www.motive.com/company/news/news_press_peregrine.html>, accessed March 21, 2001.

11. "Associates Keystone to Structure," *Discount Store News Wal-Mart Commemorative Issue,* Responsive Database Services Incorporated, 1999.

12. J. Martin, "Are You as Good as You Think You Are?" *Fortune,* September 30, 1996, pp. 142–52.

13. Ibid.

14. S. Kerr, "Risky Business: The New Pay Game," *Fortune,* July 22, 1996, pp. 93–96.

15. S. Branch, "The 100 Best Companies to Work for in America," *Fortune,* January 11, 1999, pp. 118–42.

CHAPTER 8

Instituting Quality Assurance Programs

"The product looks like the management."
—Philip B. Crosby, Quality Consultant

During the late 1970s and through most of the 1980s, the Japanese made quality a critical issue for almost all companies around the world. The message they sent was clear: "Get better or get beat!" In the United States, a number of companies were devastated by Japanese competitors who entered their markets with higher-quality goods and services. In the process, the Japanese saved global consumers from having to accept shoddy products and poor service. In fact, consumers began to demand quality in all of the products and services they purchased. The situation sparked a quality revolution that affected both manufacturing and service organizations and continues today.

Now quality is mandatory; without it companies just can't be competitive. Consumers have more choices than ever before; consequently, if a company can't deliver quality, consumers will select another company that can. By offering extremely high levels of service quality, including speed, convenience, and personalization, at a fair price (not necessarily the lowest price), many Internet-based retailers are taking sales away from their brick-and-mortar competitors.

To continually improve the quality of both new and existing business processes, a company should employ certain principles, techniques, and tools that have proved to be effective at improving quality. Simply because a business process is new or redesigned doesn't preclude its use. In fact, a company should embed these techniques and tools into its service delivery systems to ensure that those systems and their performances continue to get better over time.

Quality, Productivity, and Profits

Quality has an enormous impact on productivity and profits (see Figure 8.1). High-quality products and services help a company build a reputation for superior customer value, allowing it to increase market share and potentially charge premium prices. Additionally, quality products and services lead to customer satisfaction, which begets customer loyalty. Loyal customers ensure a solid customer base, buy more, and recruit new customers through word-of-mouth advertising, perhaps the most effective advertising method available. These outcomes have a significant positive impact on revenue generation. To achieve high product and service quality, employees must do things right the first time and every time; this reduces rework, increases productivity, and lowers warranty and liability costs as well. Consequently, companies spend less money on correcting mistakes and giving refunds to dissatisfied customers. These outcomes have a significant positive impact on reducing costs. The net benefit is greater overall profit and return on investment. In fact, winners of the Malcolm Baldrige National Quality Award outperform the Standard & Poor's 500 stock index by a factor of three in terms of return on investment.[1]

Quality and Total Quality Management (TQM)

Quality is the summation of all the product quality (performance, conformance, durability, serviceability, features, reliability, aesthetics, and perceived quality) and service quality (reliability, accessibility, communication, responsiveness, access, competency, courtesy, credibility, security, understanding, and tangibles) dimensions that a company selects as being integral to its value proposition. For example, if responsiveness (or speed of service) is an important element of a company's value proposition, then it is an important part of how the company defines quality for itself. Lesser interpretations provide little practical guidance for internal programs and activities that aim to improve quality.

The quality gurus, including W. Edwards Deming, Joseph M. Juran, and Philip Crosby, advocate various approaches for improving quality. TQM embodies their ideas as well as the growing wealth of practical experience from numerous companies. TQM is a management-driven, companywide pursuit of quality as defined by customers. It is based on a clear business direction

FIGURE 8.1
Quality, Productivity, and Profits

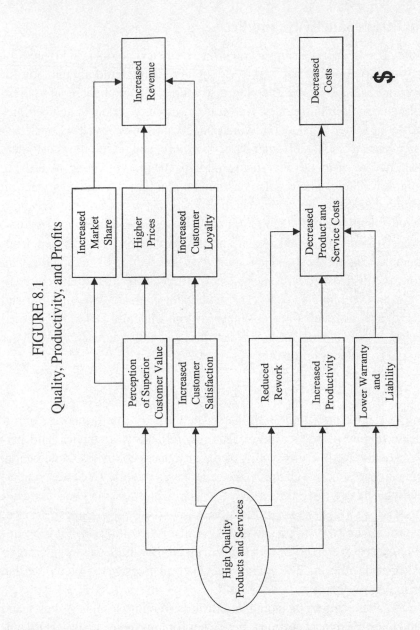

that emphasizes quality goals, objectives, and associated strategies. It incorporates policies aimed at continuous improvement. It emphasizes informed decision making based on data collected and analyzed by well-trained employees.[2] There is no one way to implement TQM: a company should develop its own version based on its interpretation of the predominant approaches (e.g., Deming's approach) and the company's unique situation. Yet all TQM efforts share some basic principles, including the following.

- Leadership—Without leadership, quality improvements don't have a chance of being accepted by and meaningfully incorporated into a company. Management is responsible for making quality a high priority in the company; providing the requisite resources (i.e., people, time, and money); and insisting that quality tools and techniques be applied on an ongoing basis. Without this level of management commitment, a quality initiative will wane as employees fail to take management seriously and over time make other priorities more important. Moreover, managers must allow employees to expose quality problems without requital and remove obstacles that prevent employees from correcting those problems. Employees have a limited radius of influence; only management has the broad reach to cross organizational boundaries and make the comprehensive changes that are often needed to improve quality.
- Customer Focus—To develop a customer focus, companies must correctly identify their target market, emphasize the importance of meeting (or exceeding) customers' requirements, and disseminate this ethos to everyone in the company, even to those employees who don't interface with customers. In companies with a customer focus, the employees know who their customers are and can articulate how their work adds value to those customers.
- Education and Training—Employees need an understanding of why quality is important and certain skills for collecting data, analyzing it, and solving quality problems. These activities require education to introduce pertinent quality concepts and principles and training to develop a common language and skill set of the most appropriate analytical tools. Employees require both generic education and detailed training. Generic education describes the logic behind a quality program, including goals, objectives, and strategies, and describes everyone's roles and responsibilities. Detailed training exposes employees to

the relevant techniques and tools for collecting data, analyzing it, and solving quality problems; demonstrates how to successfully apply them on the job; and describes how to create the policies and procedures for making them an integral part of daily operations.

- Total Involvement—Quality requires that all employees, suppliers, and partners embrace and contribute to the quality program. They must be empowered to make decisions based on hard data and take corrective action to improve a business process, their immediate environment, and the output of the process. Supportive management and a cross-functional, team-based approach foster employee involvement. However, some managers are reluctant to empower employees. This is because they haven't adequately prepared them to handle more responsibility with conviction. By providing leadership and the requisite education and training, managers can—with confidence—free employees to take the actions necessary to improve quality. Without empowerment, a company will have to continue (or resurrect) inspection by extraneous personnel and incur the associated costs.

- Continuous Improvement—Continuous improvement emphasizes that any aspect of a business process can be improved; the employees who are familiar with the process should identify and implement the improvements; and there should be constant pressure to improve the process. With a continuous improvement program, a company reduces the chance of complacency, because it is frequently elevating its performance targets and finding new ways to accomplish them.

Clearly, a focus on customers, total employee involvement, and continuous improvement can have a significant positive impact on service delivery systems. Companies that are serious about quality improvement need to embrace these principles and deploy the pertinent techniques and tools, which are required for a successful implementation of a quality program.

Quality Techniques, Tools, and Programs

Any approach for improving quality service should use one or more of the available techniques and tools (see Figure 8.2). By making them a part of a business process, a company can increase the chance of producing consistent and acceptable levels of product and service quality. Employees can

FIGURE 8.2
Techniques and Tools for Quality Programs

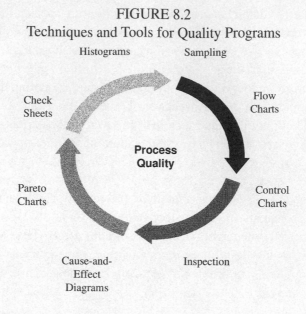

use these techniques and tools by themselves or in a group situation to solve and prevent quality problems.

Inspection is a technique used to identify nonconforming service or weed out defective products before they reach a customer or the next step in the business process. Companies can inspect a product or service's attributes, characteristics that can be counted and classified as good or bad (e.g., correctness of an order), or variables that can be measured on a continuous scale (e.g., elapsed time to a service request). One hundred percent inspection only makes sense when the cost of executing nonconforming service or passing on defects overrides inspection costs. Generally, companies use sampling to check the quality of a business process rather than perform complete inspection. With this technique, a company inspects only a portion of the process's output, thus avoiding 100 percent inspection. Sampling requires the preparation of a sampling plan, which specifies who will take samples, what should be sampled, where in the process samples should be taken, when samples should be taken (or the time interval between successful samples), sample sizes, what constitutes acceptable results, and decision rules that determine when and what actions should be taken for unacceptable results. The sampling plan may also specify the pertinent techniques and tools for collecting, analyzing, and presenting the data. Sampling makes sense when inspection costs are extremely high, or 100 percent inspection just isn't necessary.

There are a number of tools for organizing and presenting the data collected through sampling and inspection. These tools are easy to understand and apply. They play an important role in uncovering and correcting aberrant activities in a service delivery system. Some of the most prevalent tools follow.[3]

- Check sheets. Check sheets facilitate the collection of data about complaints and quality problems (see Figure 8.3). The sheets show the incidence, or frequency of occurrence, of complaints. They help answer some basic questions about service quality, such as: What are the primary complaints or problems? How often do they occur? What are the primary trends?

FIGURE 8.3
Check Sheet for Complaints

Complaints	December	January	February
Incorrect Order	160	170	186
Wrong Merchandise	7	9	9
Incorrect Package	3	5	5
Wrong Destination	10	12	12
Wrong Invoice	20	24	24
Totals	200	220	236

- Histograms and bar charts. Histograms graphically portray a frequency distribution for a particular variable. By examining the frequency distribution, companies can obtain estimates of central tendency and variation. Obviously, high variability is bad. Other tools (for example, cause-and-effect diagrams) may be employed to investigate possible causes of high variability. Bar charts portray attribute frequencies for a service or product, such as complaint or problem categories on a check sheet (see Figure 8.4).

FIGURE 8.4
Bar Chart for Complaints

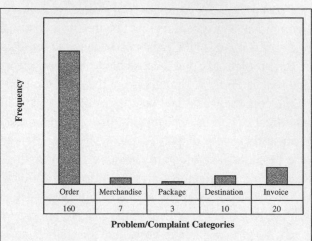

• Pareto diagrams. Pareto diagrams order the attribute frequencies from the largest to the smallest (see Figure 8.5). They demonstrate the natu-

FIGURE 8.5
Pareto Diagram for Complaints

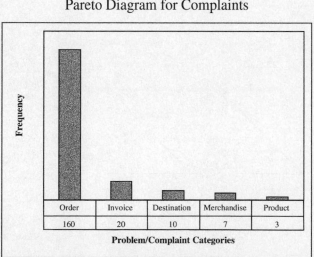

ral tendency that a majority (80 percent) of the complaints is due to a minority (20 percent) of the requisite activities. This is another version of the "80–20" rule. By isolating the primary problem activities, companies can focus on correcting them and eliminating the lion's share of complaints. A company may also want to create Pareto diagrams that portray the cost of various complaints or problems, because the most frequent complaint or problem may not be the most costly. If the most prevalent complaint is also the most costly, then the implication is obvious: fix the problem as soon as possible to improve customer satisfaction and reduce costs. When this is not the case, the company must weigh the tradeoffs between the two competing factors.

- Cause-and-effect diagrams. Cause-and-effect diagrams are extremely useful because they help display, explore, and identify the potential causes of a problem. The diagrams have a center line that unites the causes of a particular "effect," or problem (see Figure 8.6). The causes begin as general categories, including materials, personnel, equipment, methods, processes, and so on. During the analysis, employees identify possible subcauses for each category, and each of the subcauses can

FIGURE 8.6
Cause-and-Effect Diagram

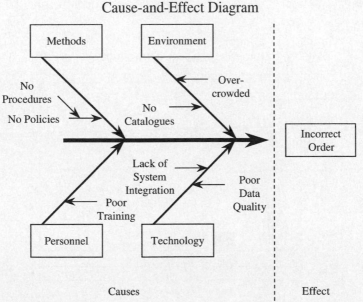

have subcauses in turn. With this approach, employees can "drill down" to specific causes that are responsible for the complaint or problem under examination; this allows the quality improvement effort to direct its efforts toward the correct areas.

- Control charts. Control charts monitor the performance of various control points of a business process over time. They have a center line, which represents the long-run average, and upper and lower control limits, which define acceptable levels of performance (see Figure 8.7). If successive samples produce averages that are consistently above (or below) the long-run average or that are tending toward a control limit, then the activity performed at the control point may be spinning out of control. Armed with this warning, employees can identify the cause(s) of the trend and make the necessary adjustments to get the process under control again.

Companies engaged in a continuous improvement program often use the Deming Wheel, or the plan-do-check-act (PDCA) cycle.[4] It is a technique that consists of four stages.

1. Plan. Employees select an activity (or method, procedure, etc.) that needs improvement, actively study it, set improvement objectives, and formulate a plan for achieving the objectives.
2. Do. Next, they implement the plan on a test basis, monitor progress, and document the results.
3. Check. Third, they analyze the results to determine if the objectives were attained. If there are major shortcomings, they may have to re-examine the activity, reevaluate the plan, or reconsider the whole project.
4. Act. Finally, if the plan is successful, they document it as a standard policy with related procedures that all employees follow.

At the conclusion of the cycle, companies may return to the planning stage and restart the cycle to continue the improvement process.

Companies that are serious about quality employ a substantive quality assurance program, which describes the policies, procedures, guidelines, and activities that define and govern quality both within and outside of their businesses. These programs incorporate many of the principles, techniques, and tools presented here. The objectives of quality assurance programs include

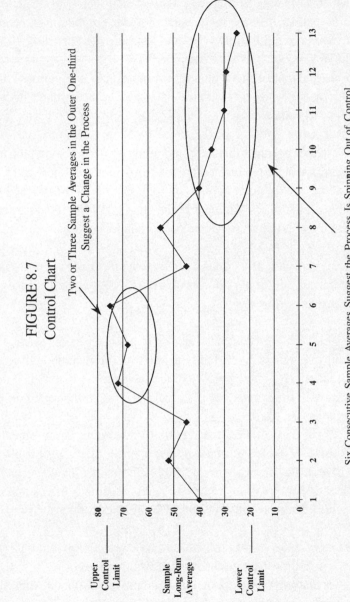

FIGURE 8.7
Control Chart

Two or Three Sample Averages in the Outer One-third
Suggest a Change in the Process

Upper
Control
Limit

Sample
Long-Run
Average

Lower
Control
Limit

Six Consecutive Sample Averages Suggest the Process Is Spinning Out of Control

147

increased productivity, greater control over quality, and reduced costs. A company that outsources some of its business processes, especially mission-critical processes (e.g., billing, customer service, and delivery), needs a strong quality assurance program to effectively manage its suppliers, because the quality of the company's products and services is directly dependent on the quality of the suppliers' performances. As part of its quality assurance program, the company should provide a supplier with the following items:

- clear specifications on cost, speed, and quality requirements;
- a quality approach for the supplier to follow, which includes recommended techniques and tools, sampling plans, and a delineation of roles and responsibilities between itself and the supplier;
- assistance in learning how to obtain error-free products and services; and
- auditing and reporting procedures so auditors and the supplier can demonstrate adherence to specifications.

The latter item is particularly important, because ongoing monitoring and audits are part of quality assurance. Maintaining uniform performance is difficult even for the best companies, thus the need for continuous monitoring activities and periodic audits.

Delivering High Levels of Service Quality at Reader's Digest

Reader's Digest subcontracts a number of key activities (e.g., order processing), preferring to keep in-house only core, proprietary activities, such as editorial and marketing activities.[5] Several suppliers conduct order processing, payments processing, and mail processing activities, which are combined into one process under the responsibility of fulfillment services (see Figure 8.8). As a recognized national brand, Reader's Digest commits to delivering the highest-quality products and services. How does the company maintain its national reputation of excellence while having a number of important services conducted out of house?

To ensure the highest possible level of customer service, Reader's Digest has a rigorous quality assurance program. Reader's Digest uses a quality

FIGURE 8.8
Reader's Digest Partial Organizational Structure

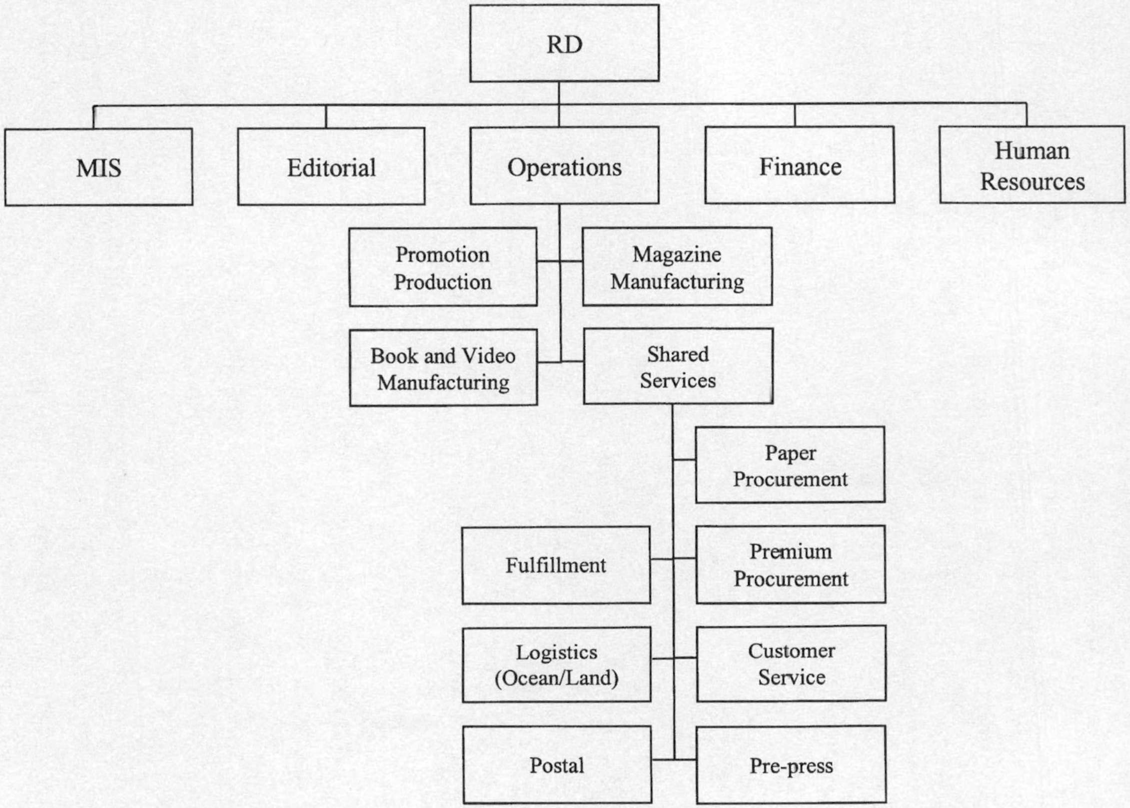

agreement, or contract, that stipulates supplier requirements relative to accuracy and timeliness. The requirements include:

- 99.5 percent sorting accuracy,
- 99.5 percent data entry accuracy, and
- 99 percent of all orders processed within two days.

Requirements escalate as suppliers implement service delivery changes that emanate from continuous improvement programs.

The company also employs service managers who are responsible for managing one or more suppliers, each supplier performing one or more activities. A service manager has a number of responsibilities, including

- selecting suppliers,
- developing and/or implementing a quality assurance program,
- monitoring supplier performance,
- training suppliers in the use and documentation of requirements for a program, and
- communicating with suppliers on an ongoing basis.

A quality assurance program describes the requirements that are important to Reader's Digest, delineates roles and responsibilities of the participants, and emphasizes the need for a supplier to maintain an effective quality management system. Reader's Digest holds all suppliers responsible for complying with and satisfying all requirements specified in contracts, purchase orders, letters of instruction, and other written and verbal correspondence. The company expects suppliers to commit to a continuous improvement program, ensuring constant improvements in productivity and customer satisfaction. Additionally, the company expects suppliers to provide periodic feedback on the quality and timeliness of inputs from Reader's Digest so that it can improve the quality of its processes as well.

To control the quality of processes, Reader's Digest advocates that suppliers use quality improvement techniques, including

- process mapping,
- inspection at control points,

- sampling,
- creation and maintenance of quality records, and
- periodic review and audit of procedures.

The objective of process control is to avoid and/or eliminate nonconforming output from every step of a process without relying on burdensome and costly final inspection.

   Quality and timeliness are the two most important service requirements, or customer specifications, because customers want their orders and payments processed correctly. The process consists of a number of activities (see Figure 8.9).

   The processing of customer correspondence begins with receiving envelopes and extracting the contents. Representatives, or "reps," perform a preliminary sort, dividing the envelope's contents into categories of work,

FIGURE 8.9
Orders and Payments Service Delivery System

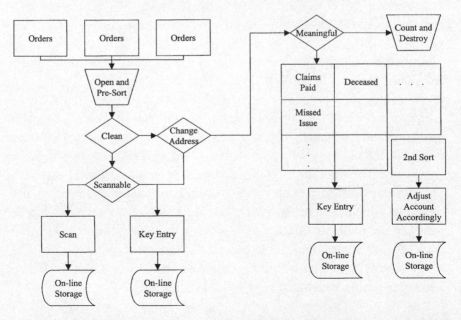

Source: This figure is a modified version of a quality assurance process described in a Reader's Digest quality assurance manual.

such as clean, change of address, and messy. Clean work is expedited, whereas messy work is handled more carefully. Reps scan clean work or, if a document is not scannable, key it into the system. They also key in change of address requests. To measure the quality of this part of the process, Reader's Digest requires suppliers to have two control points: one for scannable documents and one for keyed-in documents. A supplier's supervisors or quality assurance personnel sample batches, or trays, of documents on a periodic basis, performing a 100 percent inspection of the trays' contents. For each batch, reps complete a header slip that contains information about the batch, including unit number, batch number, and batch size. Reader's Digest reserves the right to use its own personnel to perform the sampling and inspection.

Reps sort messy documents into twenty-five to thirty other categories, including claims paid, deceased, missed issues, and a special category, second sort work. For second sort work, reps have to access customer accounts, checking account status and/or making adjustments to accounts. For the remaining categories (e.g., claims paid), reps key in the requisite data. To ensure that all work is processed correctly, Reader's Digest makes each category a control point. As with scannable and keyed-in documents, suppliers sample batches, or trays, of documents on a periodic basis, performing a 100 percent inspection of the trays' contents. For all batches, reps complete a header slip.

Each day, suppliers take a random selection of headers and check their accuracy. They maintain quality records for the sampling and inspection process at all control points (see Table 8.1). Suppliers and Reader's Digest use the quality records to monitor and measure the quality of the process at various control points and to determine whether or not suppliers are adhering to customer specifications as detailed in the contract. Supervisors and quality assurance personnel discuss any potential problems that emerge from the sampling and inspection process with various teams and individual reps. As a final step in the process, suppliers store all scanned and keyed-in data on-site for a specific length of time. At the end of each day, Reader's Digest uploads and merges all data.

Reader's Digest performs an audit one to two times per year on all suppliers. Suppliers that have trouble meeting contractual terms are audited more frequently. The company also rewards suppliers and reps on a regular

TABLE 8.1

Reporting Requirement for Sorting Quality (Sample)

Date	Time	Tray	Rep	Documents in Tray	Errors	Error Type	Work Type	QA Rep
	10:00 A.M.	157	Susan M.	2,200	11	4 messages 1 order 6 change of address	DRE—Yes	Jason H.
Total				40,000	121		99.69%	

This table is a modified version of a table described in a Reader's Digest quality assurance manual.

basis. For example, Reader's Digest will distribute certificates of appreciation and financial incentives to reps that have demonstrated exemplary performance. Other rewards include books, videos, and CDs, and company-sponsored contests and pizza parties. Reader's Digest's intent is to make all reps feel like part of the company and to act in the best interest of its customers on a daily basis, even though the activities are outsourced.

As part of a continuous improvement program, Reader's Digest expects all suppliers to make recommendations for improving the performance of the overall process. By monitoring trends in process data, suppliers can identify positive marketing and sales trends, as well as aberrant situations for corrective action. Reader's Digest also expects suppliers to propose more effective and efficient sampling and inspection plans.

Management Directives

The following management directives result from these concepts and examples.

- Don't become complacent about quality. Companies should recognize that quality is mandatory in today's world. Companies may not win orders with high levels of quality, especially in industries where it is assumed to be present, but they sure can lose them in a hurry without high quality.
- Realize that quality can improve productivity and profits. Quality leads to increased productivity, lower costs, increased revenues, and higher profits. Quality pays! It's that straightforward.
- Institute the basic principles, techniques, and tools that improve quality. To maintain the integrity of a company's value proposition and the associated service delivery systems, companies should mount and maintain quality programs. They can be full-blown TQM endeavors or quality assurance programs directed at specific business processes. Sampling and inspection plans produce data that employees can analyze using a variety of techniques and tools for identifying and correcting potential problem areas.
- Don't forsake continuous improvement programs. Continuous improvement programs maintain the pressure of getting better. Companies with such programs are constantly demanding from their employees and

suppliers better ways for improving quality, saving costs, and pleasing customers.

Notes

1. P. Port, "The Baldrige's Other Reward," *Business Week,* March 10, 1997, p. 75.
2. This definition of TQM comes from a presentation made by Professor Pasquale Sullo, Rensselaer Polytechnic Institute.
3. Only a rough description of some of the most popular tools appears here. For a more complete description of these and other tools, see any conventional quality management or operations management book.
4. Actually, W. Shewhart invented the cycle, but the Japanese attached Deming's name to it.
5. This is a particularly noteworthy example, because Reader's Digest is providing outstanding levels of customer service through numerous suppliers. With a good quality assurance program, companies can subcontract important functions with total confidence that the customer will be well served.

CHAPTER 9

Deploying Information Technology (IT)

"We see information technology as central to our ability to grow the business and create value for customers. IT is at the core of our services, and as a logistics provider, more and more information is replacing inventory or assets in the supply chain."

—John Wilson, Vice President of Marketing and Strategic Planning, UPS Worldwide Logistics

Computer and communications technologies are changing the nature of companies in numerous areas, including product and service design, sales, and distribution. The Web demonstrates how information systems can create completely new business models that change the way consumers buy airline tickets, office supplies, and a slew of other products and services. Many companies use information technology to create breakthroughs in customer value and accomplish huge efficiencies in their business processes at the same time. For example, Cisco Systems gives its customers prompt service by handling 75 percent of its sales online. Moreover, 45 percent of its online orders for networking gear never touch employees' hands, reducing cost, increasing quality, and shortening cycle times. These orders electronically flow to Cisco's manufacturing partners; as a result, Cisco's productivity has increased by 20 percent over the past two years.[1]

Information technology is giving companies the tools to develop business process innovations that provide a positive buying experience for customers; effectively link customers, retailers, and suppliers; and create more efficiency in operations. Companies without a strategy for incorporating information technology into their businesses will have a difficult time competing against the "first movers," who are innovating with information technology.

The Growing Scope of Information Systems

With information technology, companies can create customer value break-throughs at any point in the business cycle (see Figure 9.1). Information systems support customers during the process of evaluating and ordering a product or service by providing product and service information in the form of text, audio, and video; executing the payment process; optimizing fulfillment and delivery operations—ensuring reliable and timely delivery of products and services; and providing functionality for effective after-sales support and service. Consequently, the scope of information systems is broad, potentially cutting across multiple business functions, managerial levels, and often organizational boundaries, especially when a number of external partners are involved in the business cycle.

There is a growing interdependence between business direction and information technology. What a business would like to accomplish is becoming increasingly dependent on information technology. Increasing market share, becoming a leader in service, and increasing productivity depend on the information technologies that a company uses to enable its business processes and to support its customers. In fact, information technology should become an important, if not the predominant, part of a company's business strategy (certainly in the near future, given the emergence of the Web and the new business models that it has engendered).

Additionally, companies should realize that the scope of value propositions is unlimited. Information technology is giving companies the ability to communicate, create, collaborate, and control the world around them. Companies can dream up new services and then build the processes, gather the people, and implement the information systems that can deliver those services. The available technologies can do almost anything and, as a result, shouldn't limit creativity. Alcatel, the French phone giant, is providing its customers with a phone that offers touch-screen Web access. The WebTouch phones show voice mail, e-mail, and faxes on one color screen.[2] This type of service delights customers and allows the company to lock customers into a variety of other services and their associated revenue streams.

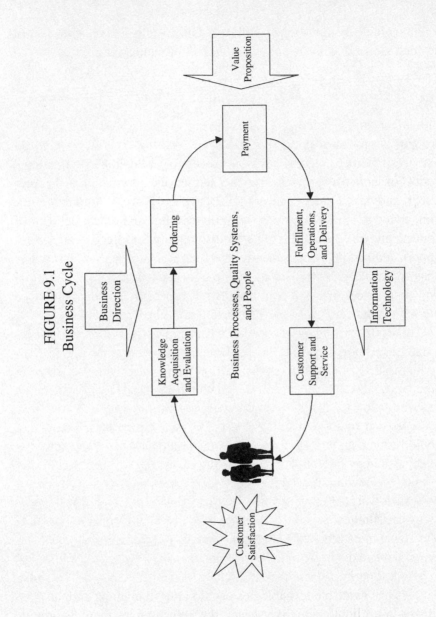

FIGURE 9.1
Business Cycle

159

Additionally, it opens the door to other innovations. For example, Geo-Vector Corporation makes software that allows phones targeting restaurants to gather online information about the restaurants, including names, addresses, phone numbers, and special offerings (e.g., free beverage during dinner).[3] These new services are just the tip of the iceberg, as one can imagine.

The core of information systems, the "crunching power" (i.e., ability of computers to log, store, and process information) of computers and network bandwidth, is increasing at unprecedented rates. Computer power has been doubling every eighteen months (i.e., Moore's Law). This phenomenon has spawned communications networks that can link devices, people, and entire organizations. In fact, communications companies are laying fiber-optic networks that far exceed current demand. The Internet and Web are creating an environment to build a multitude of new products, services, service delivery systems, business strategies, and whole companies with business models that were unimaginable a few years ago.

Improving Marketing and Sales Efforts and the Customer's Buying Experience with Information Technology

In today's world, companies need to develop capabilities that allow them to attract new customers, identify the "best" customers, retain existing customers, and offer the best possible buying experience. All these activities are related: identifying the "best" customers, rewarding them accordingly, and making the products and services they want readily available will allow companies to expand their customer base through value-added offerings and engender loyalty among existing customers, increasing customer retention rates in the process.

With information technology that collects and analyzes purchase data, retailers can identify their "best" customers (i.e., the top 20 percent, which are responsible for 80 percent of all sales) and offer them highly customized rewards. For example, in the grocery industry, a number of companies are using retail management systems to offer customers direct discounts, free merchandise, and promotional discounts on items that they use regularly. Moreover, these companies snare less frequent shoppers after they enter a store by enticing them with promotions that stimulate purchases and repeat visits. The same information technology also makes direct marketing a reality. No longer do companies have to depend on a shotgun approach to the market conveyed through flyers, circulars, and weekly advertisements. Armed with customer databases and software for detailed segmenting, customer profiling, and campaign management, companies can send marketing and sales materials to specific customers (in conventional and/or electronic form) and pursue cross-selling and up-selling opportunities. For example, using software from Net Perceptions, Amazon.com analyzes customers' purchases and suggests books, CDs, and videos that they would probably like.[4] The approach allows Amazon.com to customize service, sell additional products, and forge lasting relationships with its customers. Amazon.com also identifies frequent customers and rewards them with free priority shipping. Customers benefit because they're getting what they want and deserve, allowing Amazon.com to deliver significant customer value in the process. No longer should companies think of themselves as just selling products and services. Using information technology-enabled approaches to sales, a company can build and cement new relationships and contracts with customers. By listening to the voice of the customer through electronic transactions, a company can learn how to more effectively serve its customers.

Companies need to engineer a superior customer experience to set them above the competition. They can do this by adding value to the various stages of the typical buying process. When buying any product or service, customers pass through several stages, namely knowledge acquisition, evaluation of alternatives, ordering, and payment (see Figure 9.2). Companies can improve this process by providing information and knowledge at every stage.

By using the Web, companies are providing customers with a wealth of information on their products and services, and even their competitors's products and services. National Semiconductor allows design engineers to view products and their specifications in approximately 2,000 product folders available over the Web. The company even has customized pages for its

FIGURE 9.2
The Buying Process

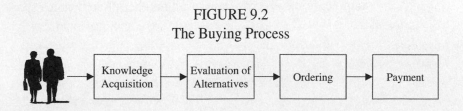

largest customers.[5] A much smaller company, Grayson Business Computers Corporation, displays equipment pictures, specifications, and pricing at its Web site. As a result, customers know what they're buying and at what prices, eliminating the need for sales literature and follow-up phone calls.[6] In each instance, the companies are providing customers with valuable information and knowledge about their products and services in a way that saves significant time (e.g., Grayson estimates that their application cuts about two weeks off the sales cycle). MicroAge Incorporated, a PC distributor that also assists companies with installation and training, goes one step further. When MicroAge is out of stock on an item, it provides data about its competitors' inventory to help customers.[7] Even though the company doesn't financially benefit from offering this information, it helps customers satisfy their needs. In doing so, the company earns customer loyalty.

Using information technology, companies are helping customers evaluate more alternatives than previously possible. Through the online community that it created, Amazon.com allows customers, authors, and publishers to share information. For example, customers that are considering a particular book can read reviews from other customers who have read the book and review comments made by the publisher and author(s). At Dell's Web site, customers can use the Configure tool to create, compare, and evaluate more than 50,000 configurations of notebooks, PCs, and servers—at least 100 times more than many of its competitors. They can compare the tradeoffs among various alternative configurations before making a final purchase decision. By finding interesting ways for sharing information and collaborating, companies can add tremendous value to their products and services.

Ordering and paying for purchases needs to be just as value-rich, although these two steps tend to be inherently more mundane relative to the previous two stages. Companies that allow customers to enter orders and have them paid with a click of a button provide the best service. Amazon.com is down to just one-click ordering. L.L. Bean's phone-based order entry system is also impressive. Customers interact with friendly, knowledgeable sales personnel who answer questions concerning availability of merchandise, prices, and shipping details, even anticipated arrival dates. When technical questions about products, such as outdoor equipment (e.g., fishing rods) need to be addressed, sales personnel quickly transfer customers to seasoned experts who can answer the questions. All merchandise can be paid for with a variety of credit cards after the order is finalized. Bean's order entry and payment process is extraordinarily easy and convenient.

Some companies handle all aspects of the buying process at exceptionally high levels (see Figure 9.3). To help customers acquire information about possible vacations, Expedia.com provides customers with the ability to roam hundreds of locations, view photographs, and request additional information about a specific site, including dining opportunities, hotels, and language. Customers can interact directly with the company via e-mail or an 800 number, seven days a week, twenty-four hours a day. Customers can obtain write-ups about locations, which adds to the sensory experience. To help customers evaluate their vacation choices, the Web site allows customers to compare the cost of various vacation packages. It also provides answers to frequently asked questions (FAQs) and travel services (for example, travel advisories). Customers can book reservations for hotels, airlines, and vacation packages at the site. Expedia.com also allows customers to create a travel profile, which the company uses to recommend customized vacation packages. Payment is equally easy, with any major credit card accepted. Expedia.com's computer-based functionality adds value at each stage of the buying process.

E-commerce hubs link buyers and suppliers to form single, efficient marketplaces. They aggregate information, including product descriptions, specifications, and prices, as well as automate basic business transactions. At a hub's Web site, buyers can quickly compare information about suppliers' products, services, and prices. For example, Chemdex.com has thousands of registered buyers and suppliers and maintains information on

FIGURE 9.3

Expedia.com's Support for the Buying Process

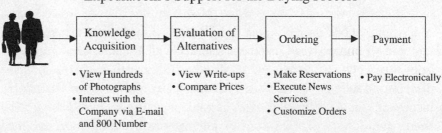

many products and services. Using the Web site, pharmaceuticals industry engineers and scientists can examine reagent prices, material safety sheets, and quality control data. The service dramatically reduces search time, and because scientists can place orders from their computers, the service cuts the cost of processing an order by over 75 percent, which is a real saving for customers.[8] In markets created by e-commerce hubs, even companies with strong brands end up selling commodities and competing on price.

If a company doesn't use information technology to improve the buying process, it risks being at the mercy of others who do. A company needs to provide customers with instant, bountiful information, even information about its competitors, or risk the chance of customers going elsewhere for it and possibly ending up with a stronger competitor. Anything less won't cut it. By empowering customers to make better decisions and easing them through the purchasing process, companies build and deepen their relationships with customers, engender loyalty, and increase sales, even in the face of infomediaries and the consequent competition. Better service isn't another nice thing to do for customers; it is mandatory.

Improving Effectiveness of Order Fulfillment, Operations, and Delivery with Information Technology

Information technology has penetrated almost every aspect of the supply chain, from purchasing at supplier locations to store operations and sales at customer, retail, and distributor locations (see Figure 9.4). Information technology can integrate suppliers', distributors', and customers' logistics systems to promote a smooth flow of goods from suppliers to a customer's home.

On the front end of the supply chain, point-of-sale (POS) technology (including scanners and bar codes), databases, and specialized software (e.g., data mining applications) allow customer service (CS) companies to collect, store, and analyze sales data. Companies can identify trends, move merchandise more effectively, and keep the correct merchandise on shelves to avoid stock outs and consequent customer dissatisfaction. Wal-Mart stores over 24 terabytes of data, which it analyzes to produce reports for store managers, identifying top-selling items by number of units sold, total dollars, and profits. This information helps stores position items—for example, at the end of aisles, where they get the proper promotion. Addition-

FIGURE 9.4

Wholesale and Retail Trade Supply Chain Activities and Related
Information Technologies

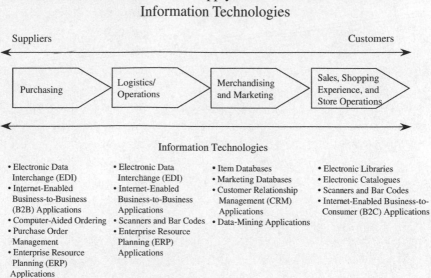

Suppliers   Customers

| Purchasing | Logistics/ Operations | Merchandising and Marketing | Sales, Shopping Experience, and Store Operations |

Information Technologies

• Electronic Data Interchange (EDI)	• Electronic Data Interchange (EDI)	• Item Databases	• Electronic Libraries
• Internet-Enabled Business-to-Business (B2B) Applications	• Internet-Enabled Business-to-Business Applications	• Marketing Databases	• Electronic Catalogues
• Computer-Aided Ordering	• Scanners and Bar Codes	• Customer Relationship Management (CRM) Applications	• Scanners and Bar Codes
• Purchase Order Management	• Enterprise Resource Planning (ERP) Applications	• Data-Mining Applications	• Internet-Enabled Business-to-Consumer (B2C) Applications
• Enterprise Resource Planning (ERP) Applications			

ally, by following unit sales at the store level, Wal-Mart can lay out an entire store to suit the demands of local patrons so only the right merchandise is on the shelves. The company also analyzes sales transactions to see how the purchases of different items are related. This information allows the company to place or market related items together. Wal-Mart is also notorious for combing the competition's circulars and responding instantly to lower prices. Managers can then offer a new lower price at their own store and contact the corporate office so that other Wal-Mart stores can be notified to roll back their prices as well. By being able to lay out a store and stock it according to the demands of the local market, Wal-Mart can offer higher service quality, adding value to its offerings and increasing customer satisfaction in the process.[9]

Many companies are electronically supporting the order fulfillment, operations, and delivery activities of the business cycle. These activities tend to be quite complicated and can involve multiple subcontractors and partners. Ideally, companies aim for a greatly integrated "pull-through" system, where highly customized products and services are pulled forward in response to customer demand and requirements. In every case, information systems are the glue that bonds the various components and players, smoothly moving products and services to customers. The systems determine what gets moved as well as when and where. For example, in response to Dell's highly effective and efficient order fulfillment, manufacturing, and delivery system, Ingram Micro Incorporated, the PC industry's largest distributor, and Solectron Corporation, a large contract manufacturer of high-tech equipment, are making custom-made PCs for PC companies (e.g., Compaq Computer), distributors, and resellers. Ingram and Solectron's system builds computers to order, keeps inventory at a minimum, reduces cycle time, and keeps costs down. Resellers transmit customer orders to an Ingram warehouse for immediate filling. If the order can't be filled from stock, special software routes it to the Ingram or Solectron facility best suited for the order. If parts are not in stock, the software immediately places orders for the missing parts to suppliers. Other systems keep the customer informed about the order's status. After the PC is made, the designated facility sends it directly to the customer or the reseller. In the existing system, the PC companies, distributors, and resellers are mainly responsible for collecting customer and PC sales data and analyzing it to learn how to improve their designs. They leave order fulfillment, manufacturing, and delivery to the experts.[10]

Wal-Mart employs advanced information technology to keep inventory under control, merchandise in stock, and costs low (see Figure 9.5). At each Wal-Mart store, POS devices collect sales data, which are used as a basis for issuing replenishment orders. Stores and distribution centers transmit the sales data, inventory position data, and replenishment orders to corporate headquarters, which analyzes it and transmits replenishment orders to suppliers. The effectiveness and efficiency of the system permits continuous replenishment of merchandise at stores and distribution centers. Wal-Mart can reduce the amount of inventory at its stores and distribution centers without sacrificing customer service, reducing overall costs and increasing the productivity of floor space within the stores.

Companies can also streamline internal processes to lower the overall cost of operations. Information technology can be used to reduce paperwork, save time, and keep employees plugged into the company. Quark Incorporated, a software developer, posts its travel policies on the corporate Web site so employees don't have to waste time searching for per diem

FIGURE 9.5
Wal-Mart Logistics System

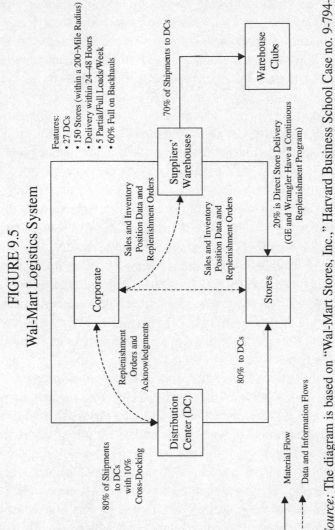

Features:
• 27 DCs
• 150 Stores (within a 200-Mile Radius)
• Delivery within 24–48 Hours
• 5 Partial/Full Loads/Week
• 60% Full on Backhauls

70% of Shipments to DCs

Warehouse Clubs

Suppliers' Warehouses

Sales and Inventory Position Data and Replenishment Orders

Corporate

Sales and Inventory Position Data and Replenishment Orders

20% is Direct Store Delivery (GE and Wrangler Have a Continuous Replenishment Program)

Stores

Replenishment Orders and Acknowledgments

80% to DCs

Distribution Center (DC)

80% of Shipments to DCs with 10% Cross-Docking

Material Flow

Data and Information Flows

Source: The diagram is based on "Wal-Mart Stores, Inc.," Harvard Business School Case no. 9-794-024, revised in 1996.

policies and other procedures. The company also makes reimbursement forms and expense reports available through their site. These applications free up employees for greater productivity.

Elevating Customer Support and Service with Information Technology

After-sales customer support and service must be at the customer's convenience, which usually means seven days a week, twenty-four hours a day. Many companies use self-help functionality because it's inexpensive and can be highly effective. Forrester suggests that Web service costs companies just $.04 per customer on average for a simple Web page query versus $1.44 per live phone call, so shifting service to the Web could let companies handle up to one-third more service queries at 43 percent of the cost.[11] When customers can find support online, they don't need to contact a call center. Self-help functionality incorporates a variety of techniques, including FAQs, which have ready answers for frequently occurring questions; key-word searches that search a database of questions and solutions; glossaries; reference libraries; and other methods that allow customers to access past experience and industry knowledge. Some companies are especially creative, getting customers to help one another. Marshall Industries makes its engineers available twenty-four hours each day through chat rooms. The company knows that customers use the chat rooms when they're in a hurry or need just one question answered. Additionally, the company's customers field questions. Marshall provides online bulletin boards where customers solve other customers' problems.[12]

AT&T's Interactive Advantage (IA) is a software system that provides customers with extensive customer support and service across their value chains, which include learning, buying, using, maintaining, and paying activities, through a standardized Web-based interface (see Figure 9.6). IA is a bundle of services that improves the value of AT&T's traditional products, including frame relay, voice/data circuits, and communication networks, and puts its products and services in the hands of its customers. All of IA's services are information-based. IA captures information from customers' telecommunications systems, makes it available to them in useful ways that helps them to run their systems and businesses more effectively,

FIGURE 9.6
AT&T's Interactive Advantage (IA)

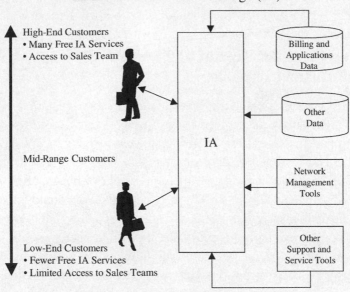

and augments it with other types of information that facilitate learning and self-help. The system also supports real-time resource allocation among the components of a network, maximizing the effectiveness and efficiency of a customer's investment. For example, via IA, customers can view the performance of a call center network, display loads at various nodes (i.e., call centers), reroute calls, and change authorizations. Using combinations of information displays and hot links, AT&T customizes a customer's graphical user interface (GUI) to provide a personalized experience for its customers. Customers see only the IA applications that are designated for them. For example, a company administrator (e.g., CIO or telecommunications manager) has a different set of pages to view than an accounts payable manager in the same organization.

IA's customer support and service features fall into eight categories of customer tools and information: Communication Center, Products and Services Information, Training and References, Network Performance, Account Information and Billing Analysis, Ordering and Status, Trouble Reporting, and Network Control. Communications Center allows customers to share information with their AT&T account team and secure discussion groups. It's an excellent method to collect customer comments, questions, and issues. Training and Reference furnishes customers with a wealth of information through a reference library and offers self-paced instruction on how to use all IA's applications. The application provides business service descriptions, on-line help manuals, and a glossary of terms and acronyms, FAQs, and primers on telecommunications technologies. With Trouble Reporting, customers can display a trouble-shooting checklist and symptoms matrixes that provide causes for various problems (e.g., can't send and receive). The application also allows customers to open trouble tickets and append a voice mail message to a trouble ticket. At an AT&T work center, technicians perform tests to isolate and correct the causes of the problems. At any time customers can obtain reports on the status of open tickets, view test results, and analyze problems encountered over time. With these functionalities, AT&T aims to have customers diagnose and solve their own problems or easily contact the correct personnel for quick resolution. Through Service Level Agreements, another IA feature, AT&T intends to help customers understand whether or not AT&T is living up to its customer support and service contractual obligations. The tool will allow customers to obtain reports that compare AT&T's performance (e.g., network) with the terms and conditions of a contract and process a credit if it's warranted.

Customized Home Pages (CHPs) is another tool that is currently under development. CHPs is primarily an information-pushing tool: a way to push content to the customer. Through CHPs, customers can obtain articles; notifications of meetings and special events; e-mail; information on their accounts; and information about AT&T's new data, voice, e-mail, and new Internet Protocol (IP) products and services. Moreover, the feature allows customers to customize the information pushed to them.

Because IA records and stores all transactions, AT&T can learn about customers and be proactive in determining how best to run a customer's business (e.g., real-time allocation of resources to minimize queues at call centers), suggesting additional products or services (e.g., pipes, switches, or frame relay), and helping customers resolve technical and billing problems. Concerning the latter, for example, customers with voice and data services can access their bills online, challenge them, and have disputes resolved online as well. Customers consider this to be a real value point. IA gives AT&T the ability to develop a relationship with customers that's based on exemplary customer support and service that is enabled with information technology.

Information Technology–Enabled Service Delivery Systems at UPS

UPS is a business that doesn't manufacture a product, but it ships approximately thirteen million packages and documents daily. To control the complexity, streamline handling and shipping operations, track packages, and deliver on time—keeping customers satisfied—the company uses a variety of technologies, including mainframes, PCs, handheld computers, and cellular networks. Together they create a vast information system for entering orders, collecting packages, tracking them, ensuring delivery of those packages, and facilitating prompt payment. The system also allows UPS to offer additional services, from electronic transmission of documents to outsourcing of numerous logistics functions, including order fulfillment, inventory control, and warehousing.

Customers issue pickup requests with the UPS Web site, a phone, or special client software provided by UPS (see Figure 9.7). The Web site allows customers to display service options, display transit times and calculate shipping and handling costs for various services to help them select the best service option, verify the correctness of addresses, and request a package pickup or determine the nearest drop-off location. The system adds orders to the schedule of the closest UPS operating center, which dispatches pickup and delivery vehicles. UPS drivers have an assigned route on which they make regularly scheduled stops. Typically, they deliver packages in the morning and pick up packages in the afternoon. The drivers carry a handheld computer, the Delivery Information Acquisition Device (DIAD), which houses an internal radio that simultaneously captures and transmits pickup and delivery information. After a driver records a pickup with the DIAD, the device relays the information to the UPS system, so that its progress to the final destination can be tracked immediately. Customers can use a phone, the Web site, and/or the client software to track the status of packages and documents using a UPS-generated reference number (essentially a purchase order number), which is attached to the package at pickup.

FIGURE 9.7

UPS Package and Document Services

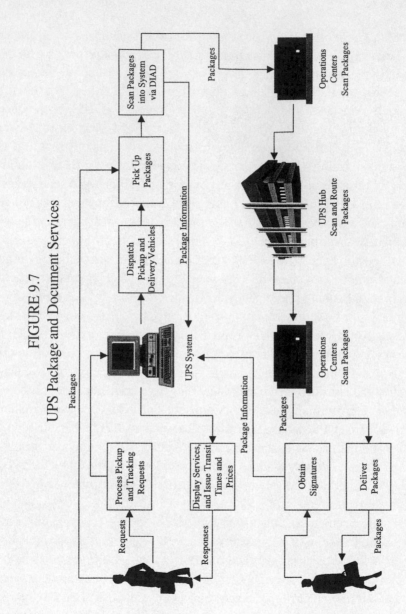

With phone service, the company's speech-enabled tracking system allows callers to simply state a package's tracking number and it responds with the date and time that the package arrived as well as the name of the person who signed for it. These features improve customer service by allowing customers to instantaneously track shipments themselves. They also reduce costs by eliminating the need to equip and staff a service center to answer basic questions and by making sure that potential for error is reduced, as faulty shipping addresses are corrected at point of order entry. UPS gets hundreds of thousands of tracking requests each day. UPS can also send a message to the DIAD about traffic jams on a driver's route or immediate pickups. This capability promotes the smooth flow of packages and helps UPS manage priorities correctly.

At operating centers and area consolidation hubs, where feeder trucks load and unload parcels, UPS equips employees with finger scanners to quickly read tracking codes. They also use automatic devices along conveyor belts for directing incoming packages to the correct outgoing loading docks for distribution to operations centers at final destinations. The conveyor system sorts and consolidates incoming packages by zip code. Before loading packages at outgoing shipping docks, employees check packages one last time, just to make sure they were correctly sorted. When a package is delivered, after a customer signs for it on a DIAD, the information is relayed to the UPS system. With the package's tracking number, the sender can determine if the package was received. UPS's information technology–enabled service delivery systems increase employee productivity, the average revenue per delivery piece, and customer satisfaction via timely and reliable deliveries.

Two data centers and a worldwide network, UPSNet, provide the foundation for the system (see Figure 9.8). The centers serve as a repository for all package and business information. UPSNet connects the company's personal computers, DIADs, and other devices that collect business data and monitor the movement of packages and documents. UPS's network can also connect to its customers' enterprise resource planning (ERP) systems via UPS OnLine Host Access, a software interface, which provides seamless integration. Customers gain access to the system using Web technology, UPS client technology, and conventional phones.[13]

FIGURE 9.8
UPS and Information Technology

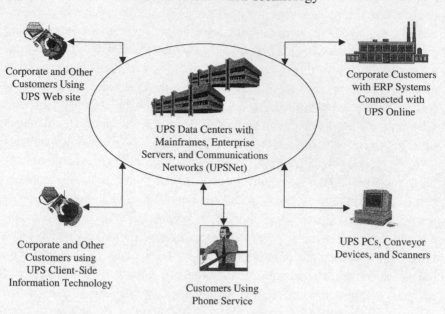

Corporate and Other Customers Using UPS Web site

Corporate Customers with ERP Systems Connected with UPS Online

UPS Data Centers with Mainframes, Enterprise Servers, and Communications Networks (UPSNet)

Corporate and Other Customers using UPS Client-Side Information Technology

Customers Using Phone Service

UPS PCs, Conveyor Devices, and Scanners

The available technologies allow UPS to go beyond its core service of carrying packages and documents. For example, UPS is capable of processing payments for its customers. UPS provides Gateway Incorporated with a cash-on-delivery service, which has UPS collecting payments from Gateway customers and depositing the money into Gateway's bank. With its DIAD, UPS can receive, validate, and securely transmit credit card payments at the point of delivery. Furthermore, UPS will make its logo available as an icon on the Palm VII, allowing a customer to enter a UPS tracking number and immediately learn the whereabouts of his or her packages. Using cellular networks, UPS can also direct customers to the nearest drop-off location, reducing search time for its customers.

In aggressively pursuing the application of information technology to improve its services and systems, UPS has developed new e-commerce and logistics services. UPS's Web site serves as an information clearinghouse for companies interested in transacting business over the Internet. The site provides customers with information on electronic solutions provided by companies, including IBM, AT&T, and Harbinger, with which UPS has strategic alliances. Each solution incorporates UPS functions, from tracking to complete shipment processing, including order entry; pick and pack; inventory management; and shipping, returns processing, accounting, and other customer service functions. Through the site, UPS provides its customers with the information and support necessary to evaluate alternatives (e.g., simple entry-level software versus advanced solutions) and make informed decisions about the best way to proceed with an Internet business.[14] UPS is now a supply chain outsourcer. For example, the company manages different aspects of the supply chain through UPS Worldwide Logistics (WWL), which is UPS's fastest-growing business. WWL is capable of handling supply chain management, warehouse operations, inventory management, transportation operations and management, and return and repair services. With its information system, WWL can also address other customer needs, such as hosting order entry, sales projections, production planning, and procurement planning activities. UPS plans to customize its solutions to specific industries (e.g., healthcare industry).[15] These services permit its customers to strengthen ties to their customers by offering world class logistics services. For example, GNB Technologies, a manufacturer of lead-acid batteries, has outsourced much of its supply chain activities to UPS. The company uses WWL to manage its shipments between plants, distribution centers, recycling centers, and retailers.[16]

Management Directives

From the previous examples, several lessons can be learned.

- Deploy information technology to enhance customer value. Information technology is largely responsible for service breakthroughs in numerous industries. Information technology can support ordering, logistics, and after-sales service activities in ways that can dramatically alter customer value. The success of many companies will depend on maintaining a delightful, need-satisfying experience for customers as they acquire information about, evaluate, buy, pay for, and receive the products and services of interest to them. Providing the customer with a positive experience through all phases of a buying cycle, from building awareness to after-sales support, is what it's all about, and technology can make it happen. Companies need to engineer a superior customer experience to set them apart and above the competition.

- Build relationships with customers. In a world where Web applications can reveal all, companies need to build and deepen relationships with customers to retain an existing customer base. By analyzing purchase, geo-demographic, and psychometric data, companies can formulate customized offerings for their customers. Providing personalized rewards, products, and services helps build lasting relationships. They can also separate "average customers" from those interested in building a relationship. The latter group may be more demanding, but they will force a company to improve its performance. Why not concentrate on just the most profitable customers?

- Substitute information for hard assets. Information technology can eliminate waste in supply chains. With access to the correct information, many companies can function with fewer people, a smaller inventory, and less space, and still deliver the highest levels of customer service and quality. Information technology can streamline and speed up processes for lower costs and shorter lead times.

- Augment after-sales support with information technology. Many companies are using information technology to engender self-help functionality, saving them money and increasing customer service in the process. Sellers and customers can learn with, from, and about each other. Yet they need the appropriate conduit. Companies can build information systems that permit two-way interaction and learning for improved support and after-sales service. By cultivating an atmosphere of openness, information sharing, and two-way exchange, company trust will grow and relationships will mature.

Notes

1. S. Hamm and M. Stepanek, "From Reengineering to E-engineering," *Business Week E.Biz,* March 22, 1999, pp. EB14–EB18.

2. P. Burrows, A. Reinhardt, and H. Green, "Beyond the PC," *Business Week,* March 8, 1999, pp. 78–86.

3. Ibid.

4. R. D. Hof, "What Every CEO Needs to Know about Electronic Business: A Survival Guide," *Business Week E.Biz*, March 22, 1999, pp. EB9–EB12.

5. K. Gerwig, "Thinking Globally about Sales Data," *Internet Week Transformation Issue*, September 14, 1998, p. 56.

6. K. Chin Leong, "Sales Teams Get Web Savvy," *Internet Week Transformation Issue*, September 14, 1998, p. 30.

7. R. D. Hof, "What Every CEO Needs to Know about Electronic Business: A Survival Guide," *Business Week E.Biz*, March 22, 1999, pp. EB9–EB12.

8. N. D. Schwartz, "The Tech Boom Will Keep on Rocking," *Fortune*, February 15, 1999, pp. 64–72.

9. C. Palmeri, "Believe in Yourself, Believe in the Merchandise," *Forbes*, September 8, 1997, pp. 118–124.

10. S. Hamm and M. Stepanek, "From Reengineering to E-engineering," *Business Week E.Biz*, March 22, 1999, pp. EB14–EB18.

11. M. Stepanek, You'll Wanna Hold Their Hands," *Business Week E.Biz*, March 22, 1999, pp. EB30–EB31.

12. P. Hood, "Who's the Boss?" *NewMedia*, October 1998, pp. 26–27.

13. D. Bartholomew, "IT Delivers for UPS," *Business and Management Practices*, December 21, 1998, pp. 58–64.

14. *PR Newswire*, PR Newswire Association, Inc., May 27, 1998.

15. D. Bartholomew, "IT Delivers for UPS," *Business and Management Practices*, December 21, 1998, pp. 58–64.

16. Ibid.

CHAPTER 10

Moving Forward

"E-commerce companies that don't provide a positive customer experience will get much less repeat business and therefore be forced out of the marketplace."
—Claes Fornell, Director, National Quality Research Center at the University of Michigan

By delivering superior customer value, companies can survive the competitive forces, including productivity, speed, and innovation, that confront them. The increasing rate of change of these forces mandates that companies move quickly to define, or redefine, customer value and build the business, personnel, quality, and information systems that deliver that value to customers. However, companies must recognize that there are obstacles to overcome, there are a few critical resources under their control, and there are no single-factor solutions for becoming successful.

Overcoming Resistance to Change

The customer value framework (CVF) provided here will benefit all companies, but it will force companies to change the way they plan their businesses, think about their customers, and manage their business, personnel, quality, and information systems. Some companies will readily embrace the entire CVF, whereas others will have a difficult time considering and/or implementing parts of it. Why are some companies more receptive than others? Why are some companies better at implementing new ideas, business systems, and technologies than others? There are several reasons for this.

In some cases, "necessity is the mother of invention." Companies that don't have a pressing need for change will become complacent. Companies

179

that are especially successful are the most likely candidates for complacency: "Why do we have to change if we're making so much money?"
When attempting to introduce new value propositions, information technologies, and/or other changes, many companies will have to overcome
complacency and the organizational inertia responsible for maintaining it.
Eventually, complacency leads to mediocrity, which will not go unpun-
ished. Bankruptcies, acquisitions, and declining profits are the mostly likely
results. Management can overcome complacency by performing an external analysis of opportunities and threats and then creating the business
goals, business function objectives, associated strategies, and work plans to
address the opportunities, thwart the perceived threats, create new initiatives, and generate movement within a company. Good managers cultivate
a sense of anxiety and create a business direction that keeps a company always moving forward. Jack Welch is famous for periodically reinventing
GE with new initiatives that improve the company's internal mechanics,
offer customers new and enhanced services, and/or provide new market opportunities for GE. He is able to introduce change in the absence of an obvious need.

In some cases, managers must persuade employees at all levels to take
up a new direction, pursue a new value proposition, and/or develop and institute new business, quality, personnel, and information systems. Why is
this necessary? Why do companies meet with employee resistance in attempting to introduce change? Some people appear to be hopelessly averse
to change. Yet humans are almost infinitely flexible. To be successful at
instituting change, a company must demonstrate that there is a relative economic advantage compared to the old approach: The company and/or employees will be financially better off as a result of the proposed change(s).
Additionally, a company has a better chance at instituting change if it can
demonstrate that the change is compatible with vested interests or results in
greater advantages for employees. A company can demonstrate financial
and other benefits by developing a convincing business case that it com-
municates to all employees and/or by demonstrating that a change will
improve employees' job performances and subsequent compensation, recognition, and even status in the company. Employees will have a difficult time
resisting new ideas that deliver more benefits to customers; change business processes, allowing them to be more productive and potentially earn

more money; and augment job-related activities with information technologies, resulting in a less stressful environment, giving employees more control over their job performances, and providing them with more decision-making authority.

Nonetheless, some employees will not embrace any changes in their daily routine, especially when it involves taking on more responsibility. Some employees have the attitude: "I don't want to make decisions, I just want to be told what to do." To address this type of inclination, a company needs to educate and train its employees beyond the task-related aspects of any job and include topics related to professional and personal (e.g., conflict management) development. By educating and training the whole person, companies are able to develop a cadre of employees who are more apt to consider new ideas, acquire new skills, and assume new responsibilities. Employees want more interesting jobs; however, they don't know about all the possibilities for enriching those jobs. Education and training can have a dramatic effect on employee motivation and morale, because it builds awareness about new approaches to work, prepares them intellectually, and gives them the confidence that they can succeed. Lack of confidence is largely responsible for employees' wanting to maintain the status quo.

However, some changes are not beneficial to employees. For example, some changes that aim to increase the effectiveness and efficiency of a business process may result in layoffs. Many reengineering projects have led to layoffs, with management having to deal with the ensuing employee resistance. This situation threatens the vested interests and income of the affected employees. To effectively manage projects with these types of ill consequences, managers must take the following steps.

1. Fully explain the need for the change.
2. Explain the outcomes of the change, including the magnitude of projected layoffs.
3. Release people all at once rather than in stages.
4. Provide released employees with assistance in seeking new positions and/or reeducating and retraining themselves.

By taking the first two steps, a company demonstrates leadership and decisiveness. By releasing people all at once, the remaining employees will not feel anxious, wondering who will be the next to go. Finally, the last step demonstrates to everyone that the company considers all of its employees to be important.

To be sure, these issues do not exhaust the list of reasons and solutions proposed to explain why companies differ in their receptivity to change and how to successfully manage change. It only touches on some of the most difficult issues often encountered.

The Critical Business Dimensions

There are three critical dimensions for improving any business: business processes, people, and technology (see Figure 10.1). If companies are going to affect customer value, it will be through the business processes they have in place, the people that work within the processes, and the information technologies that enable those processes. Fabulous new product and service ideas require operationally effective processes to make them happen. The core processes of any business can be modified to deliver more benefits to

FIGURE 10.1
Critical Dimensions for Improving
Business Performance

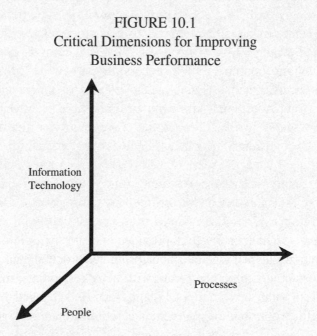

customers and/or to operate the business at lower costs. Companies can organize people in a way to provide significant value to customers through new organizational arrangements, education and training, roles and responsibilities, compensation systems, and so on. In many companies, especially service-oriented companies, people have a significant impact on customer satisfaction. Companies must manage their people in such a way as to ensure that every interaction between the company and customers is positive in nature. Finally, companies have a wealth of information technology available to them for improving customer value and business performance. Information systems have penetrated almost every aspect of a business, from customer relationship management systems that support the customer buying process, promote relationship building, and assist relationship maintenance to enterprise resource planning applications that integrate the various activities associated with making and delivering products and services.

In the late 1980s and early 1990s, Taco Bell Corporation accomplished one of the most admired and imaginative turnarounds in American industry. Based on significant customer input, the company redefined customer value as fast service, accurate orders, clean restaurants, and hot food, all at lower prices than previously offered. To provide this value, Taco Bell altered the business via the primary dimensions of business processes, people, and technology. Concerning business processes, Taco Bell completely redesigned the in-restaurant food preparation process. In the new design, restaurants performed heating and assembly activities; large centers cleaned and cooked the food. Additionally, the company introduced heating areas to hold frequently ordered items. Although the process changes significantly reduced the size of restaurant kitchens, they reduced aggregate labor costs, increased kitchen capacity, increased throughput, increased selling space, increased quality, and reduced waiting time. The company also implemented TACO (Total Automation of Company Operations), a computer and communications system that reduced in-restaurant paperwork (previously averaging 10–16 hours per week), provided managers with information on store operations, helped schedule labor, promoted production planning, and allowed restaurants to communicate with other restaurants, market managers, and corporate headquarters. Finally, Taco Bell changed the roles and responsibilities of restaurant managers and regional managers, giving them more autonomy to run the business, increasing salaries, and tying bonuses to sales performance. By using all three critical dimensions, Taco Bell was able to provide real customer value and earn solid returns.[1]

Through the many examples provided in this book, it's obvious that there are a number of options and approaches for improving a business through each of these dimensions. There are many ways to perform a process's activities; select, lead, educate, train, empower, measure, and compensate employees; and configure and deploy the information technologies available in the marketplace. Companies must continually "work the problem," devising their own approaches for improving business, personnel, and information systems so that these systems are as good as they can be, all the time.

Necessary and Sufficient Conditions

Many companies seek single-factor explanations or solutions for business success (e.g., reengineering, TQM, and the Balanced Scorecard). This doesn't work, as evidenced by the passing of one business fad after another. In order for a company to be successful at delivering customer value, it must address every aspect of the CVF provided here. Failure in any one of the essential aspects of the CVF can hold a company back, even if it has all the other ingredients required for delivering customer value. Good planning will not compensate for one or more deficient business process or an ill-prepared workforce. A solid understanding of customers' requirements will not suffice for a weak value proposition. If any element of the CVF is omitted, a company will not be able to provide the direction; value proposition; and business, personnel, quality, and information systems that are needed to get the job done.

Using rigorous internal and external business analyses, a company needs to establish complete and clear business direction (i.e., goals, objectives, strategies, and work plans) and disseminate the direction to all employees so there is only one understanding as to the company's course of action. Without clear direction, a company can develop multiple personalities as everyone develops his or her own understanding of what is (and what isn't) important, acting accordingly in what may be conflicting directions. Companies have to target the appropriate customers and exceed their needs and expectations, as communicated by customers or as inferred by managers and employees who are confident in being able to lead customers with product and service innovations that go beyond the competition's offerings. A company must amalgamate knowledge of its competencies, external opportunities and threats, goals, objectives, strategies, and customers' needs and expectations into a value proposition that will win and retain customers and earn high profits in the process. By emphasizing considerable product and/or service benefits, lower prices, or all these factors simultaneously, companies can create considerable value for customers. Soft value propositions won't stand out and be recognized by customers. Strong value propositions deliver considerable benefits to customers and save them money as well. However, in their enthusiasm to deliver customer value, companies must be careful that they don't promise more than they can deliver, disappointing customers in the process and losing their trust. Companies deliver value to customers by improving the business, personnel, quality, and information systems that underpin all value offerings.

The design of a company's business processes, the preparedness of its personnel, the integrity of its quality program, and the scope and scale of its information technology heavily affect a company's ability to deliver customer value and earn profits. Effective and efficient execution of business processes is mandatory. Business processes should include quality assurance and continuous improvement programs to ensure quality outcomes and constant improvement. Poorly designed and/or poorly executed business processes can easily prevent a company from delivering a strong value proposition and hold back a company from improving a weak one. Similarly, companies must recognize that there are many customer "touch points," where employees and/or information systems interact directly with customers. Ill-prepared employees will not be able to satisfy the customer. They'll have their own perception of quality product and services, won't be properly educated and trained to perform the requisite tasks and handle empowerment (if it's bestowed), and/or won't be properly motivated by even the best compensation systems. Finally, companies must learn how to fully support business processes with information technology and be aggressive at using information technology to create more value for customers.

Companies shouldn't be intimidated by new customer value breakthroughs developed by other companies. By adopting the CVF introduced here and applying many of the methodologies and techniques discussed in previous chapters, any company can succeed at crafting customer value breakthroughs.

Management Directives

There are several key points that managers should draw from the prior advice and examples:

- Defeat complacency. When introducing any one of the ideas presented here, managers may encounter a certain amount of "narrow-mindedness" and, in some companies, outright resistance. This shouldn't be surprising, because many companies have a tendency to become complacent over time and are reluctant to entertain any type of change. By applying the CVF presented here, some companies will need to radically alter the way they plan their businesses; learn about customers; create value for them; and manage and operate the business, personnel, quality, and information systems that underpin all value propositions. Companies can battle complacency through a combination of leadership, education and training to build competency and confidence, and demonstrate benefits that show how the business and employees are better off as a result of intended change.
- Work the problem. Business processes, technology, and people are the three key dimensions of any business. It never occurs to some managers that they can affect a business through these dimensions. However, one or more of these dimensions can be transformed in almost an infinite number of ways to increase customer value and improve profitability.
- Touch all of the bases. No one factor leads to business success. In order for a company to deliver customer value and reap the financial rewards, it must address every aspect of the CVF presented in previous chapters. Companies must establish clear direction; understand customers' needs and expectations; develop a value proposition; and build and operate the requisite business, personnel, quality, and information systems. Omitting any of these elements will prevent a company from achieving its full potential.

Note

1. The details of the Taco Bell Corporation turnaround can be found in "Taco Bell Corp.," Harvard Business School Case no. 9-692-058, 1994.

Index

In this index, page numbers in *italics* designate figures; page numbers followed by the letter "t" designate tables.